Dirty Hands

Dirty Hands

CHRISTIAN ETHICS IN A
MORALLY AMBIGUOUS WORLD

Garth Kasimu Baker-Fletcher

Fortress Press / Minneapolis

Dirty Hands
CHRISTIAN ETHICS IN A MORALLY AMBIGUOUS WORLD

Library of Congress Cataloging-in-Publication Data

Baker-Fletcher, Garth
    Dirty hands : Christian ethics in a morally ambiguous world / Garth Kasimu Baker-Fletcher.
        p. cm.
    Includes bibliographical references.
    ISBN 0-8006-3078-5 (alk. paper)
    1. Christian ethics. I. Title.
BJ1252 .B25 2000
241—dc21   00-020560

The paper used in this publication meets the minimum requirements of American national Standard for Information Sciences—Permanence of Paper for Printed Library Materials, ANSI Z239.48-1984.

Manufactured in the U.S.A.   AF 1-3078
04   03   02   01   00   1   2   3   4   5   6   7   8   9   10

Contents

Preface

My approach to teaching Christian ethics has surprised many of the students in my introductory ethics courses, especially those raised in traditional churches. For most traditional Christians there is only one approach to ethics, the so-called Bible way. I resist assuming that there is only one way to make the right choices, even in the Bible itself. I do not tell students what is right, what is wrong, or even what is the "Christian" way. Rather I try to outline an "approach" to the study of Christian ethics, or so it has seemed to many students. I talk about terms and methodologies rather than about dogmas of faith and the spiritual truth that many students expect from me as an expert in ethical analysis. Obviously, I am not the stereotypical "fundamentalist," but neither do I seem to be an "apostate." So the questions and accusations soon begin to fly. More traditional students interrogate me about my "commitment" to Christ, my "relationship with our Lord," and so forth. In so doing, they demonstrate what they consider to be genuine Christian concern for the state of my soul, my spiritual welfare. As I share my personal faith experiences, their fears for the condition of my soul are alleviated, but their expectations are not satisfied. While many claim that they "like" the new ethics professor, some remain confused about why I do not simply *tell* them how to be ethical.

What am I trying to do in these introductory courses on ethics? Am I playing fast and loose with the familiar verities, dogmas, and assumptions that are firmly anchored in some two thousand years of Christian religious thought? Why make such an effort to consider all sides of an ethical dilemma? What is Christian ethics *for*?

In our time, concerted forms of moral argumentation are often replaced by political sloganeering. Fewer people attempt to convince through persuasive forms of communication. In contrast, my approach to ethics tries to resurrect the old-fashioned ideal of communication known as "civility." There surely ought to be a way for committed Christians to communicate with each other and with persons of other beliefs without rancor. The field known as *Christian* ethics ought to begin reaching out with a renewed sense of public responsibility. Christian proclamation of the gospel will not be effective if its primary method is telling people what to believe, with little effort to persuade or listen. The ascendancy of a so-called Christian Right in national conservative politics has convinced me of the importance of articulating a more centrist orientation (or *leftist*, according to my conservative friends). To articulate a more moderate vision of Christianity than what is most commonly represented as *the* Christian response requires an approach—like the one offered in this book—to rethinking ethics itself.

Dirty Hands arises from my struggle to define such a *middle-way* Christian ethics, one that steers between the Scylla of popular fundamentalism and the Charybdis of skepticism. Such a middle way is faithful to our Christian calling to follow Jesus as Christ and also engages critical thinking about illegitimate forms of faith, government, and economics. Balancing declarations of faith with a hard-edged critical view of society is quite a challenge, intellectually and spiritually. This book aims to cultivate that skill in students by introducing the relevant terms, methods, and techniques of Christian ethical reflection.

This book also examines the fundamental ethical problematic of wanting to make good moral decisions despite the often ambiguous consequences of such decisions. How can one make the ethical and right decision in our world of deeply ambiguous morality? We are unavoidably challenged to "get our hands dirty" in the business of life, in both our private choices and our public choices, if we are to be truly engaged in sociopolitical struggle, and seek to have a positive impact on society. In our pluralistic day, and as the boundary of public and private realms becomes murky, one cannot make *any* ethical choice of action in the public sphere without offending the moral sensibilities of some, being branded "heretical" and "dangerous" by others, and being praised by still others. Such is the very nature of choice. It is public, and it is "dirty." At the same time, as Christians we try to follow a path toward holiness, sanctification, and a righteous form of living. How do we strive for moral "perfection" even as we are compelled by the vicissitudes of everyday, dirty moral decisions?

The work of *Dirty Hands* commences with the problem of moral ambiguity and then introduces the reader to the basics of ethical rhetoric and analysis. Just as a carpenter needs to know how to use tools to work with wood, so we, as ethicists, require a "tool kit" of terms, concepts, and principles that enable us to dissect and reconstruct moral dilemmas.

After outlining my constructive proposal for creating a moral landscape, or *moralscape*, I demonstrate how the moralscape can be useful in addressing specific public/private ethical issues, such as proper sexual boundaries between coworkers. By acknowledging that both private and public choices are dirty—that is, ambiguous but engaged—the idea of moralscape provides an alternative to the strong dichotomy between private moral choices and public ethos. The book ends with an extended examination of how issues of environmental justice and social justice spring from a common root in human society.

I want to thank three pre-eminent ethics professors who continue to have a profound impact on my thinking—Preston N. Williams and Ralph B. Potter Jr. at Harvard Divinity School and Katie G. Cannon at Temple University. I would also like to recognize with gratitude the mentoring and advice of colleagues: Rufus Burrows at Christian Theological Seminary in Indianapolis and Dan Rhoades of Claremont School of Theology in southern California. Colleagues like Emilie Townes, Darryl Trimiew, Arthur Dyck, and Karen Lebacqz have provided inspiration for the constructive nature of this project. Marie Fortune and Aubra Love of the Center for the Prevention of Domestic Violence have been instrumental in sensitizing me to issues of injustice toward women and children. Womanists such as Marcia Riggs, Cheryl Townsend Gilkes, Cheryl Kirk-Duggan, Patricia Hunter, Frances Wood, Delores Williams, M. Shawn Copeland, and many others have allowed me to share my ideas with them in a spirit of great warmth and supportiveness.

I am especially grateful to the students in my Spring 1997 and 1998 "Basic Christian Ethics" courses, whose constructive criticisms of earlier drafts have all been incorporated into this book. Claremont School of Theology is an exciting place to teach ethics because of its students' wide range of denominational affiliations, life experiences, and giftedness. To all of my students, *this one is for you!*

Most of all, I thank my loving family, my spouse, Karen, and Kristen, Kenneth, and Desiree, for their unfailing love and patience. Oh, that the riches of God's mercy will continue to bless all of their lives.

CHAPTER 1

The Problem:
Ethics as Orders, Dis-Orders, and a Search

The most striking feature of contemporary ethics is its often conflicting diversity of perspectives. Social ethicist Peter Paris has categorized this diversity into six influential groups of approaches, concluding that currently no consensus reigns among ethicists about which is most comprehensive, let alone most adequate. Paris's approaches can help us to understand the divisions between different ethical perspectives.

The first approaches reflect a division between a *secular-philosophical* ethics and a *theistic* or *theological* one. The next approach, *social ethics*, honors the significance of the Niebuhr brothers in the twentieth-century development of that discipline. Paris carefully delineates their importance, crediting, on the one hand, H. Richard Niebuhr's social ethics for uplifting the different ways in which Christian faith and culture interact and for recognizing the problem of religious pluralism. Reinhold Niebuhr's social ethics, on the other hand, developed through a realist model of faith in relationship to the conflict-filled arena of politics and justice. Paris's fourth approach is *liberation ethics*, a specifically social-activist, political approach, which Paris adopted in his own introductory course. Liberation ethics contrasts with a fifth approach, which he sees as a more *traditional Christian ethics*, with its emphasis on personal elaboration of doctrines and on obedience. Paris also notes that liberation ethics includes a whole host of those perspectives explicitly left out by the previous categories, including the theological ethics of African American, womanist/feminist, African, Latin American, *mujerista, minjung,* Asian, Native American, gay/lesbian, and various other formerly ignored groups. Finally, he notes that Christian ethics may be approached in a sixth way that is concerned with explicating, in various ways, the centrality of *agape,* love. Since *agape* is a central biblical category, it stands as the primary criterion of ethical choice and as the motivator for what could be called "Christian" character.[1]

How can we possibly introduce a field of study that is so diversified in its methodology that it cannot be understood as a single discipline even by its practitioners? In contrast to Paris, Dan Rhoades describes ethics as a unified field of methodological procedures for evaluating moral decision-making and actions. In his view, all the various approaches described above must be viewed as different contextual perspectives that nonetheless use the same set of academic procedures.[2] Can we agree with Rhoades that the field of ethics is, in fact, a unified discipline, or is the term *ethics* the catch-all sign we attach to any kind of moral reflection? On the one hand, even the great division in ethical practices between "religious" ethics and "philosophical" approaches has been regularly transgressed by various religious ethicists writing extended philosophical treatises. On the other hand, the unity of ethics does seem belied in practice by increased specialization. While medical students are all given a minimum basic training in what it means to be a doctor, moving on to further their training as specialists in a certain area of medical science, it seems that ethicists are trained to be specialists first, and move to a generalized training in ethical theories only if motivated by individual interest. To put it more bluntly, because there is no formal consensus on what it means to be an ethicist, because the definition of "doing ethics" is contested, students tend to learn *one* approach rather than becoming familiar with the great diversity in the discipline.

A further feature of contemporary religious ethics is the range of other relevant disciplines and considerations. Preston N. Williams insists that the best ethicists are those who are as broad and flexible in their methodologies as the multitude of concrete ethical problems they face. He encourages students to develop a view of ethics grounded on philosophical, sociological, and theological base points and to see ethics as both an *individual* and a *social* phenomenon. Thus moral choice and decision making cannot be understood unless one weds individual factors of moral deliberation, preference, and desire with social considerations of human rights, theories of justice, and an intent toward *praxis* (the technical term for *practice*).[3] The intrinsic role that sociological investigation plays in social ethical discernment is important, too, for

Arthur Dyck. His formulation of a Christian "ethic of care" stresses concern for community and how it can be preserved and nurtured.

Ralph B. Potter Jr. developed a systematic and heuristic device for analyzing the many personal and social policy aspects of ethical judgments. Affectionately called the Potter Box, it visually schematizes the ways in which norms and values interact with "quasi-theological beliefs" and views of society and how these norms and values influence our ability to filter "empirical and experiential data."[4]

We might get impatient with such diversity and complexity. But beneath this array of approaches and tools stands our unrealistic assumption that we as ethical thinkers can ever rise above all ambiguity to some peak of total clarity and correctness. We cannot clarify the parameters of the field of ethics unless we are willing to engage in the difficult task of discussing *moral ambiguity*. Acknowledgment of ambiguity, which is the absence of clearly defined and understood choices and consequences, must be at the center of the problem of ethics if ethics is to be described as a discipline at all. Ambiguity must be examined if ethics is to be a science that understands how individual persons make their choices and how they decide what is right or wrong. The same is true of society, too. We cannot make choices in the public sphere without entering into moral ambiguity and getting our hands dirty in the business of life. It is unavoidable. And if we decide that it is essential to be engaged in active sociopolitical conflict in order to change society, then our dirty hands will be examined, ridiculed, and dissected gleefully by both supporters and detractors. The unshouted business of ethics is how the inevitability of dirty hands alters both the theory and practice of ethics.

The problem of moral ambiguity is peculiarly exacerbated for a Christian ethicist because the inner goal of Christian spirituality might well be characterized as living a holy life, raising up "holy hands" because one's heart has been made holy by the cleansing power of the Holy Spirit. In this framework I would characterize Christian ethics as seeking to guide our lives toward the goal of holiness—to lift up holy hands even as we wrestle with the inevitability of getting dirty hands. Existentially and religiously, how do we help each other to grapple with the exalted goal of living into the life of sanctification while finding ways to use our dirty hands with integrity and dignity?

In light of this situation, the task of the remainder of this chapter is twofold: to describe the divergent landscape of the field of ethical study, and then to begin constructing a holistic framework that can stand as normative for a more unified vision of what "ethics" as a discipline can mean. Working toward a holistic framework means struggling to find ways to include diverse opinions while maintaining, or at least accommodating, the reality of ongoing particularities.

In attempting an inclusive definition of the field of ethics, I speak from the truth of my social and cultural particularity.[5] I seek both to affirm my particular worldview as a Jamaican-African and American Christian male and consciously to widen its constrictions by insisting that, in our postmodern "global village," our particularities must be relativized by appreciative knowledge of the multiplicity of human ethical knowledge. Thus, inclusion, so defined, is cast in a "both/and" or "diunital" fashion,[6] so that both particular loyalties and universal concerns may be affirmed. Such a diunital view of ethics is holistic rather than parochial, neither dismissing the needs of individuals or small groups in favor of an imperializing universalism that swallows up specificity, nor universalizing the peculiar dilemmas, questions, and problems of a particular group.

INVITATION TO A JOURNEY

The contemporary landscape of methodologies and approaches to the field of ethics might best be understood in three different, or perhaps successive, ways, as:

1. a conflicting miasma of dis-order (a negative evaluation of moral pluralism)

2. a startlingly new and disconcertingly complex order (discerning some underlying principle to pluralism), or

3. a kind of ongoing search for meaning, common ground, and a public voice.

It is my contention that our time requires the construction of an approach to the field of ethics that emphasizes the third way. Christian ethics is such a vast field that it must be learned as a search for meaning, for a common ground, and for a public voice. The search for meaning involves issues of faith in the broadest sense of the term.

Faith is more than a denominational affiliation, more than a frozen set
of doctrines that form a rigid framework to follow. Faith, in the sense
that the phrase "search for meaning" entails, implies a way of life, a
telic (or purposeful) journey based on certain assumptions about ultimacy, right and wrong, and the proper "end" of life. Christian ethics,
then, insofar as it can be called *Christian*, cannot be reduced to rigid
conformity to codes of obedience, duty, and fulsome reflections on following the "will of God." Rather, Christian ethics ought to be a way of
life based on the primary, vital assumption that the God of the cosmos
has been concretely revealed to humanity in the life and teachings,
death and resurrection, of Jesus of Nazareth. Such an ethics values efforts to discover the "historical Jesus," whom many biblical scholars
continue to seek.[7] By critically sifting through the ministry, life
choices, and encounters of Jesus Christ narrated in the New Testament, Christians strive to follow Jesus' way of life. This aspect of what
I will call a Journey model of ethics echoes the ancient tradition of
Christian spirituality that bases decisions about rightness and wrongness on Jesus' example, willfully acting in ways that fulfill the "proper
end" of imitating Jesus Christ *(imitatio Christi).*

For those who would call themselves *Christian* ethicists in a contemporary world of religious plurality, our mandate to present the
field of ethics as a search for meaning urges us also to move beyond
the faith parameters of Christianity. Faith is also embodied in the affective and intellectual loyalties espoused by non-theists, atheists, and
the entire spectrum of different religious affiliations in the world.
Christian ethics cannot really stand with integrity in the realm of
moral meaning unless we can appropriately and sensitively locate both
its continuities with and its differences from the ethical approaches of
other *meaning-systems,* or religions. Therefore, one essential mandate
of a constructive project in ethics is to encourage Christian ethics to
present Christian moral teachings as a meaning-system that is both
distinctive from and in certain ways in continuity with the ethical
meaning-systems of other religions.

Of the three models listed above, the "search for meaning" or Journey model of ethics synthesizes the strengths of the other two models
and eliminates their myopic focus on a single problematic—that of
whether a common moral discourse can achieve a consensus about

ethics in our era of pluralist (some would say nihilist) moralities. As one seeks to understand the ethical formations of various meaning-systems, one finds (as in the second approach to ethics as a complex order) that there is a kind of multifaceted and densely packed understanding of ethical "order" present throughout the world. Since most of us are unaccustomed to the dizzying array of moral perspectives, and to the clatter and clash of cultural norms as they bump up against one another, we tend to experience this confrontation of our moral certitudes with those of another as a "miasma of dis-order," as in the first approach. When we view this dis-order model from the perspective of the Journey model, we can see that the former actually describes our initial experience of moral pluralism and as such is like a *phenomenological approach,* while the second model seems to be more of a *descriptive-objective* or *empirical approach.* If the great questions of right and wrong, good and evil, and salvation or damnation are genuine motivators of all ethical discernment, then seeing the study of ethics as a journey is fundamental to understanding our various responses to the actual reality of various ethical systems living around the corner from each other.

The Journey approach recognizes that because most of us are raised in moral environments that are not very multicultural, multinational, or pluralist, we tend to evaluate the varieties of religious values and norms as something morally destabilizing. We may even go so far as to condemn the pluralist moral reality of the contemporary United States as a negative, secular humanist milieu inimical to the growth and development of properly Christian values. This is the strategy of many on the so-called Christian Right. Yet condemnation without genuine engagement is unacceptable from my point of view because it allows us to remain uninformed and unchallenged in a position of pseudo-superiority to other value systems. Such a strategy also reinforces an uninformed and insensitive public evaluation of all other moral discernment on important social issues because it encourages us to hear other meaning-systems, not in their own integrity, but as adversaries to our own moral position. To put it another way, without a journey or search approach to the varieties of ethical and religious worldviews, one tends to cling to one's own understanding of moral rightness and wrongness as "the Truth," condemning all others to the cellar of falsehood, heresy, and damnation.

THE MORAL LANDSCAPE

From a Journey perspective, the first step to appreciating the real dif-
ficulties most human beings have when they encounter the moral
landscape, or *moralscape*,[8] of another is to observe the array of ethical
orientations operative today (as in the first approach in the list on page
4). Recognizing the perceived dis-order in our experience of plurality
is a first step toward a much larger ethical world. Indeed, representatives of this approach have received many accolades in contemporary,
liberal, religious, moral-philosophical circles. For example, in *After
Virtue* Alasdair MacIntyre mournfully evaluates the contemporary ethical scene in an apocalyptic parable. For MacIntyre, the onslaught of
Enlightenment rationality has so emptied Western civilization of an
"objective" basis for morality that all attempts to speak of morality as
if there were still a single, unifying basis for ethical judgment remain
pitifully vitiated fragments of a formerly magnificent science. His remedy for this crisis is a turn toward a moral classicism that builds upon
a neo-Aristotelian foundation articulating civic virtues.[9]

The work of Jeffrey Stout is representative of the second position
listed on page 4—asserting that the moral landscape has reached a
startlingly pluralized and complex new order. In *Ethics after Babel*,
Stout describes the frustrations of contemporary moral philosophy in
its search for a unified moral language. Close scrutiny of Western culture reveals a diversity of moral viewpoints, which Stout perceives to
be analogous to the Tower of Babel, the biblical account of the irrec-
oncilable division of language and culture into plurality from a mythic
former unity. Yet Stout sees this pluralist situation not as worrisome or
as logically leading to an embrace of nihilism but as necessitating a
new "stereoscopic" view of morality and society,[10] a view that is more
politically realist rather than idealist. Such a view suggests a "coat of
many colors" as a new metaphor for our situation of multiple moral
languages, and it is courageous enough to patch together these complex moral components intentionally into a moral bricolage that
embraces an eclectic view of morality.[11] I call this approach *descriptive-objective* because its energies are turned to reconciling the social
data of plural moral experiences with a need for a sense of moral co-
herence. Conceptually, from the perspective of a Journey model, the

descriptive-objective approach is the second step in a process of seeking moral meaning.

⟨THE PROBLEM WITH OBEDIENCE⟩

As it evaluates various moral landscapes, a Journey model values those ethical models that do not fall so easily into either the model of disorder or the model of a complex, new order. It would value, for example, more conservative models of ethics often overlooked by many liberal ethicists, such as that of evangelical ethicists like Donald Bloesch, Oliver O'Donovan, and fundamentalist Norman Geisler.[12] Evangelical and fundamentalist ethicists take a very different approach to the objective situation of moral plurality than do MacIntyre or Stout. Citing vivid biblical allegories of a spiritual "battle" between the forces of "darkness and light" and various other images taken from the Book of Revelation as apropos to our contemporary state, some evangelical ethicists insist that a return to a traditional *obedience model* of ethics is appropriate. From their perspective, obedience to God is the single and primary norm upon which one's entire moral worldview must be constructed. The moral problem for such an ethics comes from moral worldviews that challenge with more complexity such a singularity of moral decision making. In a way, evangelical ethicists (and, most assuredly, fundamentalists) believe that all other moral worldviews and models are disordered because they are not grounded in a fundamental normativity and loyalty to God's will as expressed in Jesus Christ.

I cite evangelical ethics because my own constructive Journey model shares with them a Christian moral worldview. I believe that discerning and following God's path is the Christian's primary duty, but I am not as certain as my evangelical colleagues that one can discern God's will as a simple hard-and-fast norm. God's will can be read into situations that may or may not actually be tied to the volition of the Almighty. Even after we read Scripture and pray fervently, sometimes the most important decisions of our lives are driven more by simple desperation, loneliness, deep need for approval, or simple relief from pain. Discerning God's will involves so much more than equating my individual choice with the will of God.

The Journey model contends that ethics is the necessary enterprise of sorting out the ambiguities, contradictory loyalties, and conflicted values that face us in the messy business of everyday moral life. This messiness makes *unambiguous obedience* problematic. It is the very messiness of ethical decision making that makes ethical reflection dirty work. Calls for obedience to God seem to reduce life's complexity to a convenient set of dos and don'ts, ignoring the dirty work and suggesting that ethical choices are simply a matter of getting the correct answers (from the Bible or one's pastor) and then saying yes or no.

Ethical reflection is the serious work of getting dirty hands, even as we aspire to lift up "holy hands." Yet even with our aspirations to be holy, as we ponder which action we ought to take or not take, the most compelling moral dilemmas seem to confront us with the dirtiness of choosing between two "right" choices or two "wrong" ones. Sometimes, according to the Journey model I am suggesting, we are called upon to make the least wrong choice (say, in choosing between two undesirable political candidates) or to make the more right choice (as in choosing between two equally qualified candidates for a position of leadership). Even after making such choices, we feel the inner tug of uneasiness, a conflict rooted in the interior struggle between the messiness of moral ambiguity and the motivation to live a holy life. Obedience models of ethics seem to ignore this tension, suggesting that the tension of moral decision rests in being either obedient or disobedient.

CONSTRUCTING A JOURNEY MODEL OF ETHICS

Designing a constructive model of ethics that can journey with our stress-filled and conflictive lives requires that we recognize, up front, the fact of moral pluralism. Authenticity in our ethical choices among the warp and woof of moral plurality, it seems to me, requires a willingness to grant that other models of discernment have validity, even when I disagree with the choices that other models counsel. For example, many environmentalists believe that strong measures of "population control," implemented through the "education" of various peoples about the varieties of safe contraception, are an ecological necessity that must be instituted before further dire consequences ensue. These environmentalists advocate this course because their data indicate that the planet is being overpopulated by human beings, that human habits of habitat destruction are straining the capacities of soil, air, and water to sustain life. But such choices run counter to the religious counsels of Hinduism in India, traditional religions in Africa, and even Catholicism in Europe and the Americas. One cannot convince peoples who are religiously persuaded of the efficacy of their being "fruitful and multiplying" that their reproductive choices are actually damaging to life unless one can broach these moral differences with a respect-filled appreciation for the religious basis of their ethical choices. Therefore genuinely educated ethicists ought to understand the concrete life choices of religions or meaning-systems besides their own. Condemning others' religious practices related to sex as "satanic" or as "fornication" only serves to deepen the divide; one cannot persuade other persons to change their behavior through condemning attitudes and rhetoric. A genuine ethicist ought to be able to serve as a mediator between conflicting moral worldviews.

Gaining more than a cursory knowledge of the moral worldviews of Islam, Hinduism, Buddhism, Confucianism, Shinto, and traditional religions in various countries is a lifelong endeavor. So how can one be ethically prepared even after going through a few years of course work? Such a question deserves an answer. Most ethical training is organized by specific titles that demarcate a range of professional competence. Thus we have business ethics for business persons, medical ethics for those in the health professions, and ministerial ethics for those practicing the art of soul-craft.[2] A Journey model suggests the need for a diverse set of texts taken from various religions and fields of professional endeavor. Thus, even an introductory course in ethics for seminary students, for example, can require representative texts from the moral worldviews of business ethics, other religions beside Christianity, and medical ethics. While this task goes beyond the present work, numerous anthologies are available, and this call for a diversity of ethical knowledge can extend from the classroom to an ongoing lifelong experience of ethical learning.

Why should seminarians, for example, be compelled to learn about medical ethics? Ministers are often called to aid persons in medical crises, and most ethics courses in seminaries include some texts on various issues of medical ethics (euthanasia, life-support technology applications, abortions, etc.). Including a diverse set of religious perspectives only deepens and enriches one's consideration of such issues.

The ethics of Muslims, Jews, Hindus, Buddhists, and traditional reli-
gionists, however, is not often seen as necessary for the moral formation of a minister. In the Journey model nothing could be less helpful
than such a view.

3. Developing a Journey model of ethics requires a basic, broad understanding, drawing a "road map" of ethical models that shows the various directions that "travelers" can choose to take on their life journeys.
While it is not realistic to expect students to be familiar with all the ethical systems available, students should be able to point out ways in
which various ethical systems differ from each other. At best, a text like
this provides a methodology for incorporating knowledge of the varieties of ethical knowledge, both religious and professional. The Journey
model encourages students to deepen their knowledge of specific ethical inquiries, such as those of medicine, law, or business.

CULTURAL LOGICS. While understanding other religious worldviews
is valuable, most of us really need to gain an apprehension of our own
cultural logics, or worldview. Cultural logics are those structured and institutionalized understandings that shape our political, religious, economic, and intellectual viewpoints. They are embedded in the culture
in which we have grown up, and as such, are imprinted on us. Consciously and unconsciously, we act out of the normative standards set by
the cultural logics inscribed on our being. From the way we dress to the
patterns of speech we use, these cultural logics have an enormous influence on how we decide what is good, right, and true, as well as what
we deem bad, wrong, and untrue.

Religious worldviews, too, can be thought of as cultures with inscribed logics. For example, *Christian* ethics can be understood as
helping Christians to articulate an understanding of the kinds of Christian principles and doctrines that have been imprinted on our psyches.
Systematic theology aids us in this task, although in a Journey model,
theology is teased out of concrete ethical decision making. With Karl
Barth, I have discovered that articulating a view of the relationship between God and humanity is invariably tied to some version of a doctrine
of sin.[13] So one's views of God, humanity, and sin seem to be the first aspects of a theological articulation of one's cultural logics. The Christian
"answer" to human sinfulness is the salvific event of Jesus Christ.

Christology, then, becomes the logical next step toward articulating one's theological views. One's understanding of Christ naturally affects one's notion of church, the community of disciples of Jesus. After working out one's view of God, humanity, sin, Christ, and church, questions about the *telos*, or end, of one's life seem to come forward. I deal with these questions from within the theological framework of a doctrine of eschatology.

Cultural logics are not confined to theological or religious ideals. We cannot understand the religious or theological beliefs we share with others unless we can evaluate the political philosophy or view of society espoused in our cultural logics. The political and economic system of capitalism, for example, influences the theology of Christian believers in ways that render it far different from theologies of those living in a socialist state. The interrelationship of our sociopolitical and economic views with our religious or theological views is complex. Yet the picture is further complicated by individual factors at work in each person's life that filter cultural logics in such a distinctive manner that no two persons living in the same country, neighborhood, and even family can describe their country's and state's political, economic, and social views in the same fashion. Setting aside these complications is impossible. Finding and naming salient aspects of the web of cultural logics that influence our moral decision making is a primary task of ethics. According to Charles Kammer, understanding one's worldview (his word for what I have called cultural logics) is paramount in understanding the how and why of moral decision making.

Following Kammer's lead, I conclude that the ethical categories of loyalties, values, and norms arise in direct connection to one's cultural logics. Learning to discern and sort out our embedded cultural logics— loyalties, values, and norms—is not an easy task because it is a way of discernment that requires self-critical precision. Case studies are useful vehicles for teasing out our various conflicting loyalties, hoping that as we struggle to name our own values, greater compassion and understanding will be extended to those we encounter outside of a classroom setting.

An important aspect of any journey is the ability to rest on occasion before moving on. One cannot continually be in a state of ambiguity and dissonance, but rather, one requires moments when at least a temporary truce with ambiguity is achieved. The Journey model of ethics recognizes this psychological need as part of the ongoing process of moral meaning making. Thus, part of the journey is taking account of times when we need to press on despite feelings of discomfort caused by the dislocation of our comfortable cultural logics, as well as acknowledging when we need to rest from that dissonance.[14]

Clearly, the Journey model described thus far involves moral movement that employs both a descriptive methodology and a substantive or normative stance. While my own work advocates for wider modes of liberation, I present this broader method because it provides a kind of structure of ethical reasoning sufficiently neutral for various kinds of substantive moral stances. An evangelical ethicist can use this structure as freely as an agnostic, a conservative as successfully as a liberal.

CONSTRUCTIVE PRINCIPLES OF A JOURNEY ETHIC. Developing a Journey model of Christian ethics is a constructive discipline, seeking balance between deriving ethical norms and understanding other points of through neutral description.

Of course, one cannot present a moral stance without advocating some particular thing as "good," while judging others as "less good" or "bad." Categorizing "goods" is intrinsic to ethical reflection. Christian ethics is substantively an advocacy ethic, for its moral teachings proclaim Jesus as Christ. It advocates a particular cultural logic of rightness and wrongness. Without advocacy and its concomitant categorizing of choices into a hierarchy, decisions could never be made and our capacity to understand decisions would be rendered valueless.

Nevertheless, because ethics is also a kind of study or *science* of morality, there is also an accompanying impulse to study, analyze, and categorize as many of the possible positions and choices as are presented. This urge to understand assumes that moral reasoning can contain elements of a rationality that values objectivity. To state it another way, *the urge to understand in ethics ought to temper the urge to advocate certain positions on moral issues.* This is the important aspect of a Journey model, and it requires practice. It imposes a need to strive for rational objectivity, as one attempts to maintain the sympathizing energy of the desire to understand while also holding on to one's particular position.

While most of this chapter has emphasized a methodology for doing a Journey ethics, we cannot simply begin analyzing without articulating those embedded principles or standards of morality that are already operative in our lives. To model the practice of digging up our cultural logics, and to alert the reader to assumptions I myself bring to the journey, I ask, What positions do *I* advocate as good and right? The following is a brief outline of those principles that I hold—some general, some contextualized with social analysis, some spiritual—with the caveat that my self-awareness of all my operative cultural logics is still in progress.

Life is the arena of "moral space" from which decisions are made. We choose "this" and "not that," often without taking into account our responsibility for the consequences of our choices. To live is to make choices, and to make choices is to engage in moral activity—decision making, choosing between this or that action, and discerning rightness and wrongness. Of course, we do make many decisions that are not overtly moral, such as eating or resting. Yet even these decisions can bear moral dimensions. Not eating grapes during a boycott organized by striking migrant workers is a moral event. We create our selves and our institutions, and this self-creation is both the seat of human creativity and the expression of our moral agency.[15]

Our moral identity is rooted in what we love. We are Christians, not because we hold to a set of intellectual beliefs about Jesus and God, but because our affection, loyalties, and entire concentration of attention flow from a love relationship with God through Jesus Christ. As Martin Luther King Jr. pointed out, love is not merely a feeling, nor is it sentimental and mushy. Rather, love is a willed act of the entire psyche, animated in its whole being, energized to be wholly faithful, and exercised to the fullest degree of affective commitment. If we apply such a definition of love to the mouthings of most so-called religious people, we might find that their love exists in word only. Love moves the entire self—body, soul, and mind—to act in concert with what one believes is best for the beloved.

An ethics of love requires a deconstructive method to analyze destructive aspects of culture. The postmodernist discourse of deconstruction has tremendous usefulness as an initial tool of analysis for those interested in liberation of the oppressed. Theorists of deconstruction, such as Jacques Derrida, have been interpreted as expressing the claims of deconstruction as a substantive nihilism, and such nihilism is inimical to the substantive claims of a traditional love ethic. However, I interpret deconstruction as a humbling dynamic that makes relative the embedded idolatries of our cultural logics and functions as a necessary and powerful tool of critique.[16] Deconstruction operates in two parts: (1) critical analysis and (2) a relativizing dynamic—both of which are active in a Journey love ethic as a form of postmodern ethical discourse. As a critical analysis, deconstruction participates in postmodernity's critical distrust and suspicion of the absolutizing dynamics embedded in all cultural institutions. Deconstruction distrusts the historically demonstrated capacity of institutions to create and legitimate their power by presenting it as "truth."[17] On the other hand, deconstruction affirms the empirical reality of a radically relativized moral realm. Such radically relativized morality struggles against collapsing in on itself and becoming simple nihilism. Its critics often find deconstruction to be simply and wholly a strategy of criticism without any substantive attempt toward reconstruction.[18] As a Christian deconstructionist, I can claim the negative affirmation of deconstruction— that one must practice a habitual suspicion of ideologies embedded in substantive programs—as a necessary step *before* investigating positive implications of reconstruction. Unchecked by an ongoing methodological program of suspicion, even the grandest schemes of reconstruction can settle themselves into institutionalizations of oppressive power. At the same time, dialectically, a determined love ethic distrusts the possible return of ideology in reconstruction as it seeks to rebuild cultural, economic, and political institutions into more liberating spaces. In a very real way, the Journey love ethic suggests that deconstructive suspicion is a useful ingredient in the reconstructive energies of positing a love ethic. So conceived, deconstruction may prove to be a contribution toward reconceiving Christian postmodernity.[19]

    One peculiar bane of American cultural logics is a rampant individualism that makes it possible for Americans to lose our capacity for profound communal personhood. Such a problematic is faced spiritually in the praxis of "church," which insists that through mutual relationship with Jesus Christ the many individuals who comprise the church form the body of Christ (1 Cor. 12). *Church* is not a building, therefore, but a Spirit-filled encounter and experience of community made possible through the lived praxis of faith. Given this definition, one can see that for my own constructive work ecclesiology holds a high position since it is through church that followers of Jesus reconnect with the ancient, traditional-culture lesson embodied in the African saying, "I am because of the people, and because we are I am."

The end of a moral life, its purpose and goal, is to be connected to God, humanity, and nature. Our moral goal as human beings must never be merely an individualistic experience of the beatific "vision of God" that St. Thomas Aquinas so fervently desired. To desire a vision of God for one's self can become sinful, not because a vision of the divine is intrinsically evil, but because such a desire is inadequately motivated. It does not seek to situate the vision of God within a holistic communal context of person-in-relation to the entire cosmos—God, humanity, and all of nature (God's creation). When our end is only to die and "see God," we err, for then we have no ethical compunction to work toward better community with each other and the rest of creation. If anything, such a goal excuses us from participating in actions that deepen community, as we mistakenly "seek after God" in an individualistic mystical fashion. But our moral end is essentially connected to the life of creation; and because we are a part of nature, nature's end is invariably our own. Such a moral principle has the ethical force of a moral imperative—that we must find ways of treating all of creation as an end in and of itself, and not as means to our own individualized ends.

Communion with God through prayer connects individual persons with the entire continuum of ancestors. Such a notion stems from my reconstruction of the fragments of West African cultural logics that are operative in the kind of churches that nourished my spirituality. With a great many black followers of Jesus, I take the affirmation of our being "surrounded by" a "great cloud of witnesses" in Heb. 12:1 to include a host of unknown African spiritual leaders who add their prayers to mine every day. Further, such experience powerfully connects us with the divine, whether we are praying privately or in a group. Thus prayer is always a communal experience because it is the act that connects us with the whole host of ancestral presences, biblical and familial. Our ancestors are yet alive, and their vitality becomes real to us in prayer. I take this experience to be as real as empirical aspects of experience such as sensory stimulation.

Moral discernment must go beyond rationalist "descriptions" and involve the marriage of reason with feeling and intuitive "urges." Unlike the Enlightenment version of rational and universalizable discernment, the Journey model of discernment values a host of various measures of moral reasoning as appropriate to what might be called *moral thinking.* Reason requires affective engagement, the life of the emotions, in order to consider *all* of the options. Still, reason-feeling is not enough. Prayer is that appeal of the intuitive mind for that which is intangible, yet real. Through prayer, meditation, centering, or other forms of quieting of psyche, the internal regions of our self can come into fuller contact both with our deepest personal being as well as the Being of the cosmos. After having experienced that holy space, we are given intuitive knowledge that surpasses language and is deeper than feeling. This holy space of graced intuition urges us to move in a certain direction even when the reasoning mind cannot understand why. Yet, as can be attested by any number of different individuals, those gut instincts often turn out to be the best choices because they are connected to the Being of all rather than being merely "reasonable." Our most difficult task is learning how to marry these intuitive gut feelings to a Journey model's process of ethical self-criticism to avoid the distorted acting out of these feelings. We can learn to give our intuition breathing room within our inner holy space and at the same time to incorporate that aspect of objective reasoning that provides a cautionary word because it seeks to discern with some measure of both objectivity and spontaneity.

Love without the conjoined activity of just power amounts to an enervated praxis. This was the great ethical teaching of Martin Luther King Jr. and Reinhold Niebuhr—that love requires justice in order to be shared power, and, conversely, justice without love is merely tyrannical power.

Ultimately a love ethic trusts in God's power as constructive, positive, and meaningful. The theological basis for trusting in power comes from an understanding of God as *power-with power-sharing,* or *communal power.* Power is not a quantity to be possessed, hoarded, and guarded as a commodity; rather, it is precious because of its communal nature. God's power draws humans into deeper relationship with each other, nature, and the divine. God's power draws and attracts our attention, will, and affections. It does not coerce, because coercion is not Godly power, but merely raw domination and control.

FOR FURTHER REFLECTION

1. Utilize the category of cultural logics to describe your own church, local community, and nation.

2. Does naming ethics as the science that deals with the messiness of moral ambiguity dislodge ethics from its proper realm and role? In what ways do you agree with, disagree with, and/or go beyond this chapter's formulation?

3. Can you articulate the principles already at work in your own ethical life? How would your embedded principles differ from those detailed in the last section of this chapter?

CHAPTER 2

Obedience, Absolutism, and Real Dirt

Christian ethics has traditionally assumed that human beings can actually make completely unambiguous moral choices on a daily basis. Listen to Paul Ramsey, one of the most revered Christian ethicists: "The central ethical notion or 'category' in Christian ethics is 'obedient love'—the sort of love the gospels describe as 'love fulfilling the law' and St. Paul designates as 'faith that works through love.'"[1]

Ramsey's voice is typical of mainstream Protestant Christian ethics. Such an ethic is unambiguous and absolute in its application, for as Ramsey notes, "basic Christian ethics must itself be theory oriented toward practice."[2] When placed together, the notions of "obedient love" and "theory oriented toward practice" imply that obedience is the unambiguous means whereby God's absolute love may be revealed in a Christian's behavior. I believe that Ramsey's formulation works itself out in traditional Protestant churches as adherence to the following rules:

1. Obey the Scriptures.

2. Be guided by the Holy Spirit through faith in Jesus as the Christ.

3. Walk the straight and narrow path of salvation, not allowing one's self to be seduced, betrayed, or condemned by the sensual allurements of the world.[3]

The purpose of this chapter is to articulate the language of ethical reflection and the fundamental methodologies of ethical theory that I refer to as the ethics tool kit. After elaborating the ethics tool kit, we can explore other forms of ethics, especially non-Christian. Finally, the ethics of Dietrich Bonhoeffer, one prominent alternative to traditional Christian ethics, and compatible with Journey ethics, provides a way of undermining unambiguous absolutist ethics. As we journey, ethical dilemmas compel us to handle real dirt, to struggle with the messiness of daily moral ambiguities.

THE ETHICS TOOL KIT

Ethics is the disciplined science of critical reflection on human morality. Morality differs from ethics in our contemporary usage of the two terms. *Morality* stems from the Latin term *mores*, translated as "customs." *Customs* are culturally determined practices and traditions of conduct, views of right and wrong, that are embedded in a society. For example, in the segregated South of the late nineteenth through the mid-twentieth century, customary treatment of African Americans sometimes included lynching (torturing and hanging a person from a tree before a mob). Another aspect of this customary relationship not only expected but demanded African Americans to be servile in the presence of any white American—no matter what his or her age or social ranking. Finally, custom separated African Americans, denying them opportunities for access to any public concourse, jobs, and education with whites as a sign of their purported inferiority. These customs were accepted and practiced on a daily basis as right and fair. They were only overturned after a bloody struggle for freedom and equal civil rights spearheaded and symbolized by the ethical leadership of the Reverend Dr. Martin Luther King Jr. The demands for equal access to public facilities, educational and economic opportunities, and respect were an ethical challenge to the unquestioned customs of the time. Far from being merely complaints, or childish whining, the freedom struggle of the mid-twentieth century in the United States was a sustained, reasonable, public ethical argument for the overturning of harmful social customs against African Americans.

Ethics is carried out by reflection on rules and principles. *Principles* are "broad moral guidelines and precepts," the generalized fundamentals from which rules can be derived to provide "concrete and specific directives."[4]

Ethics helps us to discern how to negotiate conflicts or dilemmas in our loyalties. *Loyalties* are the fundamental relational ties that affectively bind us more closely to one person, group, or thing than to another. Ethical dilemmas are at root loyalty crises because at the moment of an ethical dilemma, one is being compelled to choose which person, group, or thing has a higher priority than another. A recent painful example of this was when arch-conservative Christian activist Phyllis

Schlafly, strong advocate against homosexuality as an abomination before God, had to confront the public "outing" of her son as a gay man. After much prayer and a good deal of soul searching, Schlafly was reported to have said that as a mother she would always love her son, even as she strongly disapproved of his choice of lifestyle. Such an answer reveals that Schlafly's loyalty as a mother to her son was much stronger than her loyalty to her previous rhetoric of condemnation of all homosexuals, even though she reaffirmed her ties as a conservative Christian to the anti-homosexual movement. Approaching her reply by an analysis of loyalty clarifies what might simply appear to be an inconsistent or contradictory assertion. All Christians ideally have a primary loyalty to God, even though many times our actions would belie such an assertion.

In ethical dilemmas we agonize over the conflicting values and norms that test our loyalties. Values are those "states or goods that we desire." They are the things that give our lives goals and ends toward which we strive. They give purpose and meaning to our drives. Norms, on the other hand, are the formal and informal rules and guidelines we use to embody and obtain our values. Norms are *habituated values* embedded in what we take to be our loyalties. Values and norms interact, and they need to be analyzed together. They function in a way analogous to another pair of ethics terms, *ends* and *means*. In Greek, *telos* is the "completion, fulfillment, or end" of something. Values move toward a *telos*, driving toward the completion or embodiment of a goal. The means are the choices one makes, the ethical practices and the moral example one embodies on the way to a *telos*. For example, one of the primary sociocultural values in the United States is material success. Some Americans (particularly corporate leaders!) believe that since the *telos* of life, its ultimate goal, is material success, then any means whatsoever for achieving that goal are acceptable, even illegal activities or the immoral exploitation of other people and their labor. The emphasis on increasing the bottom line of economic profitability can be understood in ethical language as the imposition of a new norm of success wherein concern for the welfare of one's employees is displaced in favor of increased profitability. While most U.S. citizens still vigorously uphold the traditional American value of success, increasingly we hear the hue and cry of moral denunciation of the regnant norm of crass profiteering that not only strips employees of their job security but also threatens their domestic stability.[5]

In ethical argumentation, two basic approaches can be used—the deontological and the teleological. *Deontology* refers to norms derived from a fixed being or nature of things (*ontos* is Greek for "being"). Deontological arguments stress duty and adherence and obedience to one's intrinsic "responsibilities." Deontological arguments do not consider possible consequences as an aspect of the process of moral decision making but posit certain prima facie absolutes or exceptionless norms, which hold, regardless of situation or context, to be the proper basis for promoting a certain position as right or wrong. Deontologists take their absolutist arguments to be part of *natural law*, the laws that God has embedded in all of creation. For example, deontological arguments against abortion usually regard the commandment "Thou shalt not kill" as the prima facie absolute that is violated by the act of abortion.

Teleological arguments, in contrast, are based on a *consequentialist ethic*, which is grounded on a view of the *telos* or sought-after good that is understood to be an end. The most popular form of teleological ethics that most contemporary persons are familiar with is *utilitarian ethics*, a teleological ethics based on the principle of the greatest good for the greatest number. Teleological arguments are based on a culturally determined, or sometimes religiously determined, understanding of a "good"—whether it be happiness, equality, freedom, justice, or some other prized social value. A teleological argument about abortion would weigh the social pros and cons of abortion and of the prohibition of abortion to decide whether abortions ought to be performed or not. It would look at nonmoral factors and sociological data, as well as religious beliefs about abortion. Ever pragmatic, the teleological approach emphasizes decision making that attempts to gauge future consequences of a choice rather than adhering to or obeying a fixed principle, as in deontological arguments. It is the strong emphasis on consequences that makes teleological ethical reflection anathema to the claims of prima facie absolutes that deeply inform the moral argumentation of deontologists.

Christian ethics may also be understood as a *koinonia ethics*, an ethical vision based on the impact of the Christian community (in Greek: *koinonia*). Christian ethics is a koinonia ethics inasmuch as it promotes an ongoing relationship of faith in Jesus as Christ.[6] The *koinonia* emphasis stresses the formation of character and virtues. *Character* is the name given to the moral being of a person or group as it has been distinctively constituted.[7] Character is the product of what Bruce C. Birch and Larry Rasmussen call the moral legacy of our communities—for good and ill. The term *moral legacy* may be another way of speaking about *customs* or *ethos* because moral legacies are "passed on" from older generations to younger ones in "traditions and rituals people practice, stories they tell, and the songs they sing."[8] For example, since much of our contemporary life is typified by the casual abusive violence that has permeated media and artistic creativity, the character of contemporary life is casually violent, even as efforts are made to control and diminish the levels of violence in society. It is important to recognize that the moral development of the community is not wholly determined by the negative aspects of the community's moral legacy. While a moral legacy (or customs, or ethos) is embedded in our collective social fabric, as individuals we can also selectively internalize particular aspects of our community's moral legacy while being free from others. This selective internalization allows individuals to act in ways that are more ethical and honorable than the community standard, and this can temper the determinism inherent in the notion of a moral legacy.[9] In any case, for Christians like Birch and Rasmussen, the community is most assuredly the "chief architect of character," while "character is the chief architect of our decisions and actions."[10] Finally, character is comprised of dispositions and intentions. *Dispositions* are the ongoing and "persisting attitudes" that recur consistently in our conduct. *Intentions* are those particular "expressions of character which show *aim, direction*, and *purpose* . . . thus revealing our *volition* or will." *Will* is a metaphysical term used by philosophers, like *mind* or *faculty*, but in Christian ethics it remains an important aspect of our Ethics Tool Kit. *Volition* is an aspect of both *moral agency*, or the ability of a self to think, decide, and act from a sense of being a "moral actor" (*agency* comes from the Latin root *agere*—to act), and *moral being*, or our moral character as described above.

Virtues, on the other hand, are important aspects of character because they are those qualities or "excellences" that characterize the moral agent judged to possess a "good character." More will be said about virtues later.

WHICH COMMUNITY—CHURCH OR SOCIETY?

Which community is most influential to Christian character formation, the church or the rest of society? Christians have struggled throughout history with this question, trying to describe the proper relationship between the church and the so-called world, outside of the influence and moral teachings of Jesus Christ and the Holy Spirit. Even as early as St. Paul, metaphors were used to describe a kind of duality, or doubleness, in the Christian life. In Romans, chapters 7 and 8, Paul expressed the ongoing tensions between the ethos of the "flesh" and that of the "Spirit." Augustine described this tension in a metaphor (borrowed from Plato's *Republic*)—Christians abide on the spiritual plane of the "City of God" while struggling to obey the political commands of the "City of the Earth," sometimes described as the "City of Perdition."

Martin Luther, building on Augustine, developed a *two-kingdom ethic* in which life is radically bifurcated into "the kingdom of God" and "the kingdom of the world." Sometimes he used the imagery of two swords, the "secular" and the "spiritual," to represent these two forms. The kingdom of God is ruled by the norm of Christ's love, spiritually disciplined and guided, privately and individually discerned between believers and God (and therefore not a publicly recognized institution or "church"), and ever in a state of blessedness. Luther understood the kingdom of the world as eternally torn by conflict and debased in a propensity to sinful violence, from which it must be constrained. From this Luther concluded that the God-ordained usage of the "secular sword" by a political sovereign is properly sanctioned to provide the means of violence necessary to restrain the vicious violence and murdering instincts of the "mob." Since Christians live in the world, their bodies "belong" to the secular authorities, but their personal hearts, faith, and minds belong ultimately to the kingdom of God. Therefore, according to Luther, Christians ought to serve without hesitation in the world as executioners, soldiers, and anything else necessary to fulfill what he discerned as God's command for order in the secular world.[11]

While the two-kingdom ethic tackles the problem of Christian involvement in the affairs of secular humanity, its radical bifurcation of the Christian life suggests an unhealthy duality. Certainly Paul's anguished

cries at the end of Romans 7 let us know that it is difficult to follow
Christian standards of compassionate, loving conduct. But in his solu-
tion, Luther marched Christians off to wars and violent suppressions of
so-called enemies of the state. Such an ethic even led to a kind of political quietism that the uncompromising Christian movement of earlier
centuries may have found horrifying. Luther would have Christians
getting their hands dirty in the most violent forms of suppression of anti-
state resistance, potentially turning freedom-fighters of the soul into actual armed police! Yet Luther was doggedly rejecting what he took to be
a dangerous form of Christian *antinomianism,* which literally means
"against law." An antinomian viewpoint rejects all commonly held ethical norms and values[12]; Luther saw such a tendency in certain An-
abaptist sociopolitical doctrines of the time that seemed to undermine
Christian obedience to the temporal law. Both Augustine and Luther
believed that the strong call for submission to worldly authorities en-
joined in Romans 13 makes it impossible for Christians *not* to embrace
some form of dual-obedience model. To put it another way, while attempting to promote the absolute holiness of a Christian world and to
constrain mob violence and sinfulness, Luther and Augustine both
wound up promoting various forms of violence.

DECONSTRUCTION AND VIRTUES. A Journey-model critique of the
two-kingdom ethic deconstructs the need for one sole norm of moral
conduct, that is, obedience. Since both Augustine and Luther define
obedience as the sole norm of ethical conduct, they are compelled to
find ways around the demands for obedience by earthly powers and authorities when they conflicted with scriptural/church-based demands.
The norm of obedience is not enough; sometimes we need to look toward developing the *cardinal virtues,* or the "four moral excellencies"
that Thomas Aquinas speaks of: prudence, temperance, justice, and
fortitude. Aquinas holds that these virtues are a good that express the
golden mean of moderation between excess and deficiency. Thus fortitude or courage is a golden mean between the excess of rashness and
the deficiency of a panicked cowardice—something any good soldier
would want to exercise on the battlefield.[13] Yet while developing the cardinal virtues is a distinct good for Aquinas, they are not enough in
themselves for human beings to be "saved" or potent enough to grant

what he considers the grand *telos* of life—a beatific vision of the Divine. What is necessary for this *telos* is faith in Christ, which according to Aquinas provides the ability to receive the *infused virtues,* otherwise known as the *theological virtues* of faith, hope, and love.

POINTS OF DEPARTURE

Part of becoming acquainted with the tools of the ethics trade is being able to recognize the components and characteristic concerns of various models of ethical reflection. By gaining access to the Ethics Tool Kit, one may gradually work toward mastering the concepts, identifying their traits in daily situations and conversation. It is important to know these terms in order to appreciate the diversity and tensions inherent in the many points of departure that initiate and sustain ethical reflection.

Our points of departure radically affect our capacity to examine the landscape of moral reality, or *moralscape.* Antagonistic religious claims not only permeate the substance of a group's ethical stance but also influence the methodologies chosen for presenting that stance. For example, because most conservative religious groups (Christian or otherwise) adhere to an *absolutist* framework of understanding ethical duties, choices, and acts, they also tend to choose methodologies that stress duty and obedience. On the other hand, more liberal views on religious dogma (Christian or otherwise) tend to view the substance of belief from a *pluralist* view, which attempts to consider the multiplicity or variety of religious and ethical choices, and they thereby choose methodologies that stress the relativity and consequences of decisions. An absolutist framework is built on the notion that there are *fundamental commands* or *principles* that provide the basic outlines of proper moral choices for life. The pluralist weighs ethical principles against other factors, such as history and social context. Thus, our ethical points of departure are also influenced by the host of *social factors,* such as class, ethnic or racial background,[14] nationality, and personality type, that make us the complex human beings that we are.

David Clark and Robert Rakestraw rightly call attention to three levels at which ethical reflection takes place. The primary level of ethics is the *descriptive* level, which seeks to portray and describe moral actions, decision making, and principles. The second level is *normative* or *prescriptive;* here the descriptions produced at the first level are evaluated—the moral actions, decisions, and virtues at hand are judged as right or wrong. Christian ethics has traditionally been strongly prescriptive. The most general and abstract level is that of *metaethics,* which seeks to analyze the second level, clarifying the meaning of ethical terms and critically assessing the ethical principles on which argumentation is based.[15] In a way, metaethics might best be thought of as *theorizing about ethics.* Clark and Rakestraw use the example of "sacrifice" in three ways to demonstrate each level: "Do most people act sacrificially? is a descriptive question. Is self-sacrifice good? is a normative question. How do we know self-sacrifice is good? is a metaethical one."[16]

The twentieth century in the West has witnessed the flourishing of two approaches to ethical reflection that radically contrast with the traditionally prescriptive approaches of Christian ethics, the approach of *positivism* and that of *emotivism.* Positivism defends descriptive approaches while disparaging prescriptive ones as meaningless expressions of a *noncognitive* or emotional nature.[17] Emotivism is a particular form of *positivism.* As espoused by A. J. Ayer, emotivism vigorously proposes that all ethical statements are fundamentally emotional expressions. For example, take the prescriptive statement, "Abortion is evil." Emotivists would insist that the phrase "I hate abortion!" adequately expresses the underlying meaning of the statement, while the positivist would note that the former statement cannot accurately articulate objective moral reality.

Both positivism and emotivism are strong versions of *ethical relativism.* Ethical relativism obtains at all three levels—descriptive, prescriptive, and metaethical. The weakest form of relativism is *descriptive relativism,* which simply observes that, given the variety of cultures and historical forms in the world, different peoples hold a wide divergence of moral beliefs and practices. Clark and Rakestraw, though Christian prescriptivists, note that descriptive relativism appears accurately to describe the diversity of moral beliefs and practices in the world. *Normative relativism* goes further, holding that apparently contradictory beliefs may both be right because of their relative appropriateness in different cultures. The strongest form of relativism is *metaethical relativism,* which insists that "principles of justification and concepts of moral values are legitimately different for different persons, religions, or cultures," say Clark and Rakestraw. For them, metaethical relativism precludes the possibility of making cross-cultural ethical judgments, and so they strongly condemn it as an approach that is ultimately contradictory and inimical to a Christian ethics.

The moralscape also includes three alternative visions of Christian ethics, which appeared in the mid-twentieth century. From Karl Barth and Emil Brunner arose *divine command ethics*, an absolutist imperative that all ethics are derived from God's will. Divine command ethics stresses the norm of obedience to God's will, and as such, agrees with other forms of *absolutist voluntarism* wherein decision making occurs by conforming the human will to God's will.[18] Barth's absolutism was nontraditional, however, in the sense that it refused to offer specific moral guidance, and thus he was sometimes criticized for being "occasionalistic."[19]

The second approach was *Christian realism*, arising from the large and varied corpus of Reinhold Niebuhr's writings. Niebuhr's Christian realism stressed a normative dialectic of love and justice as necessary to the ongoing conflictual processes of public policy making. Christian realism always turned to a critical dialectic of society vs. the individual. That tension demanded Christian ethics to maintain ongoing vigilance toward ethical positions. Niebuhr's "realism" enjoyed a widespread influence in part because of his popularity in the radio and press media of his time.[20]

H. Richard Niebuhr, Reinhold's brother, provided a third, albeit less well-known approach—that of *relationality-responsibility*. H. Richard's work called for greater awareness of the relational context in which ethical persons are called to act on norms in the most fitting or apt response to others. "Fitting action" is the action that flows from a relational consideration. It anticipates not only a singular reaction to one's decision but the conscious and sensitive extension of responsibility to the whole range of possible immediate responses, including possible future responses.[21] Such an ethic is invariably consequentialist, even though H. Richard Niebuhr saw himself as overcoming the tight limitations of the teleological and deontological approaches.

For the last three decades, *liberation ethics* have flourished. Spurred by the historical struggle for civil and human rights in the United States, black liberationists like James H. Cone have sought to counter the historic tensions of slavery and dehumanization with the "liberating and empowering Gospel of Jesus Christ." By critically interrogating Euro-American Christian practices of racism and exclusion, Cone injected theological meaning and ethical significance to Blackness, transforming it from a mere sociological category to one worthy of the intellectual endeavors of religious thought. In Latin America, at virtually the same moment in time, Gustavo Gutiérrez and others were calling on the Roman Catholic Church to embody the radically humanizing dimensions of the Second Vatican Council. Their liberation theology redefined the parameters of salvation to include sociopolitical and economic deliverance. Feminist liberation ethicists like Mary Daly have produced devastating critiques of global forms of institutionalized male power—patriarchy—that have a detrimental effect on the humanity of women. Each of Daly's works, from *Beyond God the Father* (1973), to *Gyn/Ecology* (1984), to *Pure Lust* (1988), has taken further steps toward *thealogical* construction (that is, religious reflection centered on female aspects of the divine), necessarily distancing itself progressively from those categories of patriarchal thinking deemed irrelevant or damaging to women. Gay and lesbian persons like Mary Hunt, Renee Hill, and Elias Farajaje-Jones have recently begun to create a similar critique of the oppressive norms of *heterosexism*—the conscious or unconscious oppression of all forms of sexuality not heterosexual and the erasure and even violent subjugation of homosexuals.

Liberationist ethics grows out of a particular experience of oppression that then provides fertile ground for critique, upon which an alternative vision of human flourishing can arise. Recently, *ecological ethics* is considered a liberationist program for the deliverance of nature from oppressive human polluting practices. *Process ethics* has joined the ecological ethics and liberationist ethics movements, informed by a powerful contemporary cosmology—that of Alfred North Whitehead. Process cosmology marries a trenchant critique of Western "substantialist" thinking to a stress on both the continuities and the inevitable variations in time and space. Whitehead was interested in developing a modern version of the notion—held by the ancient Greek philosopher Heraclitus—that reality is typified by change. Process ethicists like David R. Griffin and John B. Cobb Jr. seek to find ways of speaking about the "preservation of value" necessary for the reconstruction of the ecological environment.[22]

Further deconstruction of Western ethics can be seen in the work of Cornel West. He has provided an excellent ongoing critique of the crassly materialist and media-promoted sensationalism that typifies contemporary First-World existence. His ethical analysis is a critique of hedonism—"pleasure is the only positive value and pain or 'unpleasant consciousness' the only thing that has negative intrinsic value. . . . All other values are derived from these two."[23] Ironically, West asserts, continual seeking after pleasure creates the *hedonism paradox;* pleasure-seeking is inherently insatiable.

MODELS AND THE ROLE OF SCRIPTURE

Traditional Christian ethics may be understood as representative of an *obedience model* of ethics. A traditional obedience model of ethics is characterized by a prescriptive approach, an emphasis on absolute ethical commands, and dependence on a norm of obedience to these commands. The Journey model of ethics I suggested in the previous chapter differs from the obedience model because it attempts to make persons aware of their embedded cultural logics, ethos, and moral legacy while striving to expand that moralscape through an active openness to new empirical data from other moralscapes. A Journey model represents a *via media* or "middle-way" Christianity, located between the extremes of conservative Christianity and radical atheistic humanism. While maintaining with the obedience model that the Holy Spirit does efficaciously mediate our ethical decision making, a Journey model makes facile descriptions of how the Spirit has led one to decide *this way* rather than *that* problematic. Further, a Journey model undermines the unfounded assumption that one may go about "obeying Scripture" in a literal fashion, or, as the slogan goes in many evangelical and fundamentalist churches, "The Bible says it, I believe it, that settles it."

Rather, a Journey model insists upon using the Bible as the most authoritative source of Christian life. In agreement with the Wesleyan Quadrilateral, Methodism's four parameters of discernment, the Journey model holds that the authority of Scripture must be balanced with the authority of tradition as explicated in the historical teachings of

Christian churches, their theologies, and Christian ethics. *Reason* is another authority whereby human beings can make critical discernment about the applicability of scriptural texts. Reason in scriptural studies stands for critically using the historical tools of the biblical scholars. As a middle-way follower of Jesus Christ, I am compelled to weigh the arguments of those who are charged with the responsibility of interpreting ancient biblical texts by using the tools of their discipline. Between fundamentalist literalism and ultra-liberalism's absolute disenchantment with supernaturalism and its debunking of the Bible lies the carefully discerned, middle-way Journey hermeneutic (theory of interpretation) of Scripture.

One cannot hope to achieve the balanced Journey space between the extremities of fundamentalism and ultra-liberalism unless the fourth aspect of the Wesleyan Quadrilateral is employed, that of *experience*. Experience allows us to integrate our personal spirituality of a daily prayer life with the rigorous demands of critical and historical research into ways in which the Bible has been translated and understood previously. To encourage prayer is to assert the point that spirituality affects moral agency. It is to insist that spirituality can open moral decision making to the influence of the Holy Spirit. One cannot engage in prayer as an efficacious aspect of moral agency if one does not believe that the Holy Spirit can be experienced. In a rationalized age, ironically, both fundamentalists and ultraliberals seem uncomfortable with the "strangely warmed heart" (John Wesley) of middle-way Christianity. Both extremes seem more comfortable with rationalizations about why "experience" can lead to "emotional excesses" (according to the ultraliberal) and "dogmatic dangers" (according to the fundamentalist). Within a Journey hermeneutic of the Bible we embrace rigorous criticism through reason, balanced by an ever-growing knowledge of tradition and the personal empowerment of experience with God's Holy Spirit.

Such a hermeneutical model is inherently ambiguous. Application of this model must be disciplined in two ways: one, in our daily devotional practices before God and others, and two, in pushing ourselves to become more informed about the Bible's historical settings and communities and to discern as faithfully as possible the original intentions of the author(s) of particular biblical passages. This Journey hermeneutic is open to deconstructive questions about the original *Sitz im Leben* ("situation in life") of troubling biblical passages that support violence, homophobia, and the horrors visited on women because of the pervasive patriarchy present throughout biblical history. For example, understanding Lot's historical context (Gen. 19:1-11) does not mean one must approve of Lot's decision to offer his two daughters to a violent crowd of men in Sodom—even if such a moral decision could be understood as a customary way of being a "good host" in that city. A Journey biblical hermeneutic would probably condemn Lot's choice as immoral, even finding ways to affirm the angelic punishment meted out against the crowd.

Ambiguity is difficult, I dare say maddeningly frustrating, to live with. It is much easier to literalize our reading of Scripture and then let the chips fall where they may, as do fundamentalists, or, as the ultraliberal seems to do, to explain everything away as fanciful "tales" whose value is limited by their historical particularity. A Journey hermeneutic of the Bible takes seriously the injunction of 2 Timothy 2:15, "Study to show thyself approved, a worker that need not be ashamed, rightly discerning the Word of God." When we take seriously the claims of historical-critical scholarship of the Bible, our hands get dirty with the problems of the people of Isaiah's time, Paul's time, and Jesus' time even before we dig into the messiness of our own contemporary moral quandaries. With our minds informed by the best research available about the historical contexts and meaning of biblical texts, we can reach out to make ethical choices, earnestly desiring holy hands and righteousness.

THE CENTRALITY OF AGAPE

The theological notion of God's unconditional, sacrificial, and efficacious overflowing love—*agape*—lies at the heart of most ethics that call themselves Christian in any sense of the word. While I shall elaborate the theological implications of various views of love in chapter 4, it must be simply stated that one of the few things different Christian ethics share with each other is a central place for a view of God's love, and how that love operates to guide, influence, and transform human decision making.

NON-CHRISTIAN ETHICS

Since we have established that a Journey model of ethics also ought to consider non-Christian sources and materials, we must look at the ways in which ethics is practiced outside of the Christian tradition. Ethicists have recently become more acquainted with a *comparative* model of ethics, which seeks to set the ethical traditions of various religious traditions side-by-side for comparison, descriptive analysis, and appreciation of both similarities and difference. S. Cromwell Crawford, for example, provides an excellent comparative model of religious ethics, examining the basic moral doctrines, ethical practices, metaphysics, and sexual, social, and political issues important to each of ten world religions. Crawford's examination includes a detailed description of the cardinal ethical principles of each religion. For example, in Hinduism the Sanskrit word for "ethics" is *dharma* (from *dhar,* "to hold"). Dharma is a very holistic and fluid concept, encompassing a dynamic idea of law, customs, and religious practices. In fact, dharma represents "activity [and] mobility, and is possessed of catalytic qualities," and could be compared with the Western concept of *natural law* (which Aquinas defined as "the objects to which men have a natural tendency . . . among such tendencies it is proper to man to act according to reason."[24]) Its opposite is *a-dharma,* or "stasis, stoppage."[25] Likewise, in Islam the notion of law, or *Shari'ah,* is also central. However, unlike dharma, Shari'ah cannot be understood without a fuller explanation of Islam's essential religious truths, including the purpose of humanity, human innocence, and the duties of a devout Muslim. Shari'ah is "a complete system of desiderata, principles, rules, and laws regarding human activity" in which human moral actions are classified into different categories: obligatory (*wajib*) and recommended (*mandub*); prohibited (*cheram*) and recommended against (*makruh*).[26]

In Judaism the centrality of Torah makes for a fascinating comparison to the Christian norm of God's *agape* expressed in the life, death, and resurrection of Jesus Christ. In the Matthean account of Jesus' baptism by his cousin John the Baptist (Matt. 3:13-15), Jesus insists on completing the baptism as an act of righteousness (*tsedakah* in Hebrew). Jesus, as a righteous Jew, insisted that his teaching followed and even fulfilled both the "law and the prophets" (*Torah* and *Nebi'im*) in his

Sermon on the Mount (Matt. 5–7). Torah consists for Jews in both adherence to obligatory duties and commands (*haggadah*) and walking in
righteousness with God (*halakah*).

A further relevant dimension is the rise of postmodern thought and
its ethical stance. Zygmunt Bauman has systematically articulated this
less-than-systemic trend, which is critical of the traditional assumptions of much religious ethics. Postmodern ethics, as expressed particularly by Bauman in his review of the thought of postmodern philosophers Jacques Derrida, Jean-François Lyotard, and Michel Foucault,
can be summarized in seven key convictions:

1. *Human beings are morally ambivalent; ambivalence resides at the
heart of the "primary scene" of human face to face.* The contradictory
assertions "Humans are essentially good, and they only have to be as-
sisted to act according to their nature," on the one hand, and "Humans
are essentially bad, and they must be prevented from acting on their impulses," on the other hand, are both wrong. Moral conduct cannot be
"guaranteed," nor can humanity create better contexts for better morality. Rather, "we need to learn to live without such guarantees—that a
perfect society, as well as a perfect human being, is not a viable
prospect, while attempts to prove the contrary result in more cruelty
than humanity, certainly less morality."[27]

2. *Moral phenomena are inherently nonrational.* Ethics is considered after the pattern of law, which relies on regularity, repetition,
and monotonous predictability—all things that moral phenomena cannot be.

3. *Morality is incurably uncertain or aporetic.* Since few moral
choices can be understood as "unambiguously good," and even a singular "moral impulse, if acted upon in full, leads to immoral consequences . . . ," the genuinely moral self must learn to feel and act in the
context of ambivalence "shot through with uncertainty."[28]

4. *Morality is not universalizable, but this does not lead to an utter
relativism that degenerates into nihilism.* Rather, the ethical universalizing that postmodern thinkers find in modernity is a "thinly disguised
declaration of intent to embark on . . . an arduous campaign to smother
differences and above all eliminate all 'wild'—autonomous, obstreper-
ous, and uncontrolled—sources of moral judgment." The modern age
has substituted "heteronomous, enforced-from-the-outside" rules for

autonomy, leading to nothing less than the "incapacitation, even destruction, of the moral self." For this reason postmodern ethicists condemn the universal project of modernity as "the silencing of moral impulse and channeling of moral capacities to socially designed targets that may, and do, include immoral purposes."[29]

5. *While appearing irrational to the order of modern rationality, postmodern impulses provide the "raw material of sociality and commitment to others, in which all social orders are moulded."* Instead of being outlawed or suppressed, these impulses need to be tamed and harnessed in the moral self, to be kept trim and "in a desired shape without [the moral self's] growth being stifled and its vitality desiccated." Performing this delicate and complex task, societal institutions of "social management" contribute to a deepening, rather than a lessening, of moral ambivalence.[30]

6. *"Given the ambiguous impact of societal efforts at ethical legislation, moral responsibility*—being for the Other before one can be with the Other—*is the first reality and starting point rather than[the] 'product' of society."* Morality is therefore a kind of "ultimate, nondetermined presence" and a mystery that defies reason. By demanding that one relinquish self-interest, moral responsibility is the act of self-constitution, since it leads the moral self toward becoming a social self.[31]

7. *Postmodern ethics, by exposing "the essential incongruity between any power-assisted ethical code on the one hand, and the infinitely complex condition of the moral self on the other," reveals the "relativity of ethical codes and of moral practices they recommend or support to be the outcome of the politically promoted parochiality of ethical codes that pretend to be universal."* Thus any "humankind-wide moral unity is thinkable . . . [only] as the utopian horizon" that deconstructs the "deluge of claims of nation-states, nations-in-search-of-the-state, traditional communities, and communities-in-search-of-a-tradition, tribes, and neo-tribes, as well as their appointed and self-appointed spokesmen and prophets." Thus, postmodernity holds out a universal moral unity as only a "remote prospect of emancipation of the autonomous moral self and vindication of its moral responsibility."[32]

In a very real way postmodern ethics builds on the *humanist ethics* of such philosophers as Friedrich Nietzsche and Bertrand Russell in deconstructing any and every heteronomous authority (even, and perhaps most especially, God) and calling for humanity to take an ultimate responsibility for itself. Christian ethics has much to learn from and contribute to postmodern approaches. One finds anticipations of a Christian postmodern ethics in the life and work of Dietrich Bonhoeffer.

DIETRICH BONHOEFFER'S ETHIC OF RADICAL GRACE

A Journey ethics refines itself by remaining open to challenges, and the ethics of Dietrich Bonhoeffer offers an excellent example of such openness. Renowned as pastor, theologian, and seminary professor, he was also one of those few German Christians who opposed the Nazi regime. He got his moral hands dirty by helping to develop an alternative German Christian church—the so-called Confessing church—and eventually he joined a conspiracy of fellow anti-Hitler resisters (the *Abwehr*) to assassinate the Führer. How could a Christian of any sort deliberately plot the murder of another human being, even if that particular human being was the horrific moral monstrosity named Adolf Hitler? What kinds of norms and values are operative when a Christian feels compelled to act in such a way? Bonhoeffer was arrested, confined to a concentration camp, and eventually executed. In this way he died for his faith, like many earlier Christian martyrs. Can Bonhoeffer's choice be a model of Christian holiness? Is his choice of martyrdom worth emulating, or should we repudiate his choice as too dirty?

I believe that it is possible to construe Bonhoeffer's radically contextualized view of ethics by looking at both his early work and his view of grace. In his 1929 lecture "What Is a Christian?" we can tease out certain revolutionary ethical themes that not only have postmodernist implications but also transform traditional Christian ethics in a subversive fashion. In this lecture, Bonhoeffer sets out to strike down authoritarian pretensions to an "objective" view of God's grace, calling instead for a daily sense of the "presentness" of God's moral guidance through grace. Bonhoeffer notes that "the Holy Spirit is only in the present, in ethical decision, and not in fixed moral precepts, in ethical principles."[33] If taken literally, such a statement would seem to be antinomian and utterly situational. But by decrying the rigidity of making ethical decisions based simply on "principles," Bonhoeffer seeks to drive the listeners toward his true goal—daily moral renewal. Instead of an enervated adherence to the process of reasoning through ethical principles, Bonhoeffer calls for "a direct relationship to God's will . . . ever sought afresh." Moral decision making, like all aspects of one's relationship to God's will through the Holy Spirit, becomes a radical daily act of consecration: "I do not do something again today because it seemed to me to be good yesterday, but because the will of God points out this way to me today. This is the great moral renewal through Jesus, the renunciation of principles, of rulings, in the words of the Bible, of the Law, and this follows as a consequence of the Christian idea of God: for if there was a generally valid moral law, then there would be a way from [humanity] to God."[34]

This challenging daily moral renewal brings the individual Christian into a profoundly heroic solitude before God that Bonhoeffer believed was the real "higher person" (*Übermensch*) portrayed in Nietzsche's poetic philosophy. The Christian higher person "creates new tables, a new Decalogue," that defy "time-honored morals" in favor of doing the bidding of God's will. Further, this doing awakens within the solitary self a profound "consciousness of being called, of being claimed by God." Bonhoeffer believed that this profound calling also isolated the called person from others, drawing the called self into responsibility by God, for God, and to God alone.[35]

It is at this point in Bonhoeffer's address that he makes his most startling claim, one that rings prophetically in light of his decision fifteen years later to conspire against Hitler. Bonhoeffer claims that in this solitary relationship with God, "face to face with God, I can only know for myself, completely personally, what is good and what is evil." Indeed, he says, "There are no actions which are bad in themselves—*even murder can be justified* [emphasis mine]—there is only faithfulness to God's will or deviation from it."[36]

It would be easy to condemn such moral reasoning as theologically unsound, or as the early ramblings of a not-fully-formed ethic, but to do so would be to miss Bonhoeffer's underlying emphasis on human faithfulness as the proper response to whatever God's will demands. More than fifteen hundred years ago, Augustine of Hippo also tackled the related issue of Christians participating in a "just war." He insisted that a war could not be considered "just" unless it was declared by the recognized sovereign political authority, had a just cause, had a reasonable chance of being won, and was waged through proportional (not excessive) means. Like Bonhoeffer, Augustine emphasized the need for a faithful response to the gruesome ethical dilemma of participating in war. Bonhoeffer's position, therefore, is not completely out of sync with traditional Christian ethical traditions.

In later writings, such as *The Cost of Discipleship*, we find Bonhoeffer modifying the rugged individualism before God he articulated in the earlier lecture. For the later Bonhoeffer, faithful living out of God's will needs to be done in the community context and *praxis* of Christian discipleship. Criticizing the official German Christian church not only for caving into Nazism but also for legitimating it with theological justifications, Bonhoeffer contrasted the "cheap grace" of the German Christian church with the "costly grace" of the Confessing church. Cheap grace, for Bonhoeffer, is "Grace without price, grace without cost . . . sold on the market like a cheapjack's wares."[37] Ultimately estranged from the genuine graciousness bestowed by Jesus Christ and untested in the rigors of discipleship, cheap grace is worthless because it is "the grace we bestow on ourselves."

Costly grace, in contrast, "is the gospel . . . to be sought again and again, the gift that must be asked for, the door at which [one] must knock." Such grace is costly to God, as it comes through the suffering and incarnation of the Son of God. It is costly to us because it "confronts us as a gracious call to follow Jesus."[38]

One can only attain the blessing of costly grace by following a strict norm of obedience, that is, belief in Jesus and following that belief. Such obedience became Bonhoeffer's central norm and enabled faithfulness to God's call.[39] Even though Bonhoeffer named it *obedience*, this call to faithful following emphasizes the costliness of one's moral journey rather than merely reinforcing thoughtless and easy conformity to what other persons command one to do. It is a radical alternative to the authoritarian obedience we criticized early in this chapter. Bonhoeffer's obedience is not the same as opening up one's heart to a narrow list of faith statements (cheap grace) but demands daily reconsecration and discernment of God's calling in one's life, even at the cost of one's reputation, or even one's life.

Bonhoeffer's ethics reveals the need to revise and recast Christian ethical traditions. Built into the very fabric of his ethics are dirty hands trying to be holy hands, calling Christians to authentic living in perilous, dangerous, and lethal times. Faint-hearted and sentimentalized visions of a mild-mannered Jesus being followed by hosts of sheeplike followers is not what Bonhoeffer believed to be an ethic of costly grace, discipleship, and faithfulness. Rather, through the solitary experience of God's call and the responsibility such a call entailed, as well as through the community-nurtured context of discipleship, one forges a faithful though costly response to God's will that leads one to dirty one's hands in concrete works of social justice. Many contemporary North Americans live in situations far removed from the ongoing terror of Nazism, so such a rigorist ethic may seem extreme, out of place, and irrelevant. Yet engaging in dirty hands will prove costly. Bonhoeffer proved his faithfulness unto death by being willing to take the awful/awesome responsibility for his decisions, ultimately dying in a concentration camp next to the same Jews he had hoped to help liberate through the death of Hitler. Most cannot and will not follow Bonhoeffer's example, be they Christian or not. His is indeed an ethic for the courageous, for those freed from the fear of death.

IMPLICATIONS OF BONHOEFFER'S ETHIC
FOR A JOURNEY (MIDDLE-WAY) ETHICS

As a journey affords new vistas on familiar territory, so a Journey ethics of middle-way Christians can find ways to revise both itself and traditional Christian ethics. Following are six elements of this reformation. 1. *Obedience can be recast as an aim toward faithfulness and discipleship.* Bonhoeffer's insistence on faithfulness challenges a Journey ethic to recognize that faithfulness is being fiercely loyal in one's values to following God. Following God's will, then, does not aim at mechanically conforming to rules, but demands a rigorous form of discipleship. Discipleship is not acting out mindless and mechanical applications of the gospel as if being a Christian is acting ethically with strict legalism. Rather, discipleship involves *the costly, daily exercise of faithfulness in following Jesus.* In times of great injustice and violence this kind of following may even entail the possibility of death. Yet the *telos* of discipleship is not death but the bringing forth in the name of Jesus the "abundant life" of God as experienced through the Holy Spirit.

2. *Moral ambiguity and anti-authoritarianism cannot be dismissed by Christian ethics.* A Journey model, while understanding the need in traditional Christian ethics for obedience as the proper aim of a Christian life, recognizes that in reality moral life is riddled with ambiguity. Even while trying to remedy certain social evils, we participate in the unwitting creation of other (sometimes worse) evils. In Christianity, *the radical claim of God's authority subverts all other authorities*; to neglect this truth would dilute the power of Christian anti-authoritarianism. Finding ways to affirm Christian values while recognizing the fact of ambiguity and learning to celebrate the Christian contribution to anti-authoritarianism make a Journey model of ethics far more tensive, restless, and dynamic than traditional models.

3. *We can revise our understanding of God's presence in daily ethical decision making.* If we say that the aim of obedience is faithfulness to enacting God's calling in our lives, we are left with the question "How can we discern that will?" Is God's will written forever in the Bible, so that anything else one might "feel" must either have a direct corollary in the Bible or be dismissed out of hand as "not from God?" We revise our understanding of how to be faithful to God's will by *recognizing the experience of the Holy Spirit acting in our hearts as central to the process of ethical discernment.* Experience is a valuable aspect of the Wesleyan Quadrilateral discernment process discussed earlier. Asserting the centrality of religious experience of the Holy Spirit is not without problems, because many contemporary Christians have either dismissed the presence of the Holy Spirit as "emotionalism" or smothered it in various stylized cultural forms of praise, bodily movement, and impulsive behavior. To affirm that one can experience the Holy Spirit requires renewed practice of daily prayer, meditation, centering, and quietness before God. Just as God creates each of us differently, so experiences of the Holy Spirit's operation within human hearts are vastly different from one person to another. Nobody can tell anybody with iron-clad certainty what the Holy Spirit "feels" like. Such a statement is irrational, or at least nonrational, but is theologically informed and ethically sound.

4. *Liberating praxis arises in the community context of discipleship.* Discipleship requires giving to others, but it also requires an ability to receive from others. This give-and-take is a human modeling of the

interaction of God within God's self, the community of God tradition-ally symbolized by the Trinity. Each member of a discipleship commu-nity both gives to others and receives from others. This is how grace flows within the community, and discernment of the Holy Spirit's call-ing on our individual lives is checked by the fruits our lives bear within community.

5. *We gain deeper insight into the will of God by encouraging fellow-ship and communion between ourselves and the rest of God's creation.* What this boils down to is a thorough reworking of our understanding of nature, a recognition that creation is an *abode of God's Spirit.* Sometimes we need to imitate Jesus by doing just as Jesus did when he took time to pray to "the Father." He would go off by himself, climbing up a mountain, turning aside from the settled paths of human civilization to commune with God in nature. Human beings are a part of nature, so communing with nature enables the kind of prayer that reconnects us with the wholeness of creation. God's cre-ativity operating in nature supports us in our quest to "hear" and ex-perience God's presence.

6. *We embrace difference as a gift of God.* Theologically we affirm God as the great artist who delights in creating difference—in hair tex-tures, skin coloring, hue, body types, and so forth. Just as no two flow-ers are exactly alike, God the artist has fashioned no two individuals (even in the same family) to be exactly alike. As such, difference is the-ologically inscribed into the fabric of all creation. Human beings, under the impact of various universalizing and imperialistic (sinful) ideologies, have smothered difference with shallow versions of "unity," making dif-ference an enemy of "progress." Instead, a Journey ethics must take a stand to affirm the intrinsic value of even major differences in humans and in human society, just as we already do in the rest of nature.

I have not tried to make critical remarks about every single tech-nical phrase, movement, or ideology in ethics. Instead, I have pre-sented the middle-way Journey ethics as a model that builds on vari-ous currents of postmodernity, such as anti-authoritarianism and ambiguousness, while at the same time it finds ways to affirm more traditional notions of obedience (strongly revised) and discipleship.

FOR FURTHER REFLECTION

1. Do you agree with the normative criticism in Journey ethics, namely that traditional Christian ethics has emphasized obedience to the exclusion of other norms?

2. How do faithfulness and discipleship address the problem of moral ambiguity?

3. Could you institute a middle-way Journey model in your church? If so, why? If not, why not?

CHAPTER 3

Journey Moralscape

One of the most difficult moments for those who seek to find the Moral and the Good is discerning *how* and *why* we make the decisions that we do. What are the parameters of our choices? Are they predetermined in some vague sense by a mysterious mixture of things such as upbringing, community, and environment? Or are most of our decisions based on our personal and individual capacity to reason responsibly despite our upbringing, environment, and community? That is, to what extent do the decisions we make mirror our environment, upbringing, and communities, and in what ways are we distinctively individuals, understanding and reasoning morally outside of our environmental conditioning? Is there a way to discern which aspect—moral legacy or individual choice—is more influential in our everyday decision making? Or do we fall into a misleading reductionism by even considering the problem to be one of environment vs. individual responsibility? After all, human beings are emotional creatures. Is it not true that we often seem driven by the way we feel at a given time? Can these emotional states have an inordinate influence on our capacity to determine right from wrong? When we widen the paired questions of how and why we decide as we do to include other variables such as emotions, bodily health or disease, economic interest, or even the weather, we begin to glimpse the vast complexity of moral reasoning. How and why we decide as we do can become a cosmic question, sending us on a many-sided quest to nail down intellectually what cannot be easily captured or described.

Even though the process of our moral reasoning is so complex, puzzling, and rich with the potencies of chance and whimsy, ethicists attempt to provide structured models to describe it. The Journey model of ethics suggested in chapter 1 builds on the formative work of Ralph Potter, Daniel Maguire, and Charles Kammer III, beginning with a detailed description of how the moral landscape or *moralscape* of human beings operates in daily decision making. The concept of moralscape provides a rich metaphor capable of revealing to our intellects the endless complexity of human moral reasoning. Even beyond its heuristic and metaphorical power, the moralscape model can be successfully applied to everyday analysis of common moral dilemmas—a flexible tool in our own lives and in helping or teaching others. As a landscape suggests a panoramic view of several geographical points, such as mountains, wetlands, and a body of water, so moralscape suggests that there are observable phenomena or elements of human moral formation that can be described and analyzed. Further, the concept of moralscape developed in a Journey model wrestles with the tangled complexity of moral reality that I call the dirty hands of life. So doing, the Journey model constructs a process of moral reasoning that radically undermines the somewhat facile arrogance of traditional obedience models, as was mentioned in chapter 2. It is an aid to the discernment at the heart of ethics.

HISTORICAL DEVELOPMENT OF MORALSCAPE MODELS

Among the observable phenomena of a moralscape are certain dominant elements that may be ordered into a model of some sort. Kammer's work on moralscape significantly develops the formative work of the Potter Box introduced in chapter 1. Since the Potter Box remains one of the most important tools for contemporary ethicists, we need to take a few paragraphs to describe both its strengths and weaknesses. Developed as a critical tool with which to analyze public policies during the Vietnam War, the box elaborates four general areas employed in the complex process of moral reasoning (see Fig. 1).

These four elements comprise an interlocking system of critical reflection, each influencing, limiting, and reinforcing the other. Kammer, however, apparently detected a rigidity and sharpness in Potter's distinctions between the categories, and one senses that this rigidity may have prompted him eventually to modify Potter's version of the box. It is important for us to know Potter's own definitions since they form the basis for a Journey model. For example, for Potter, to formulate an empirical definition of a situation is not merely to state what one takes to

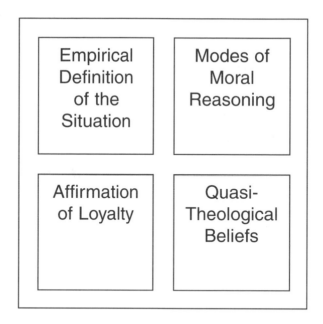

Empirical Definition of the Situation	Modes of Moral Reasoning
Affirmation of Loyalty	Quasi-Theological Beliefs

FIGURE 1. THE POTTER BOX[1]

be the pertinent facts, but also to make judgments and predictions of possible future outcomes. Likewise, our affirmation(s) of loyalty are those conscious and also unconscious decisions we make to uphold our primary object of concern, thereby expressively symbolizing our center of value, locus of commitment, and source of identity. Potter describes the modes of moral reasoning in a series of questions regarding how we make the choices we make, including the component priorities and factors we deem pertinent to such decision making. The fourth element in the box, the so-called quasi-theological beliefs, are not only our unspecified beliefs concerning God, humanity, and human destiny, but also specific "anthropological assumptions about the range of human freedom and [humanity]'s power to predict and control historical events."[2]

The strength of the Potter Box is that it provides an analytical model suggestive of the process of moral decision making. The power of any model is its ability to suggest a larger range of ideas than are present in the actual model. It is clear that we human beings base our choices on what we take to be the actual facts of the situation; that our loyalties provide powerful centers of value affecting our decisions—consciously or not; that we use various modes of reasoning to justify and rationalize these decisions; and that we are also influenced by our beliefs about divinity, humanity, and how freedom can be realized. All of these elements seem to click with us as we read them. The question remaining is whether or not the box describes enough of the moralscape. Its suggestive power is challenged by our need.

The primary weakness of the Potter Box is that it fails to elaborate clearly the relationship between the four elements. Several problems arise from this lack of elaboration. For example, Potter's categories direct us to investigate deeper psychological and socially embedded levels of human moral process within the elements of loyalties and quasi-theological beliefs, but Potter does not name these deeper levels or incorporate them into the box. While emotional or affective bonds are suggested by loyalties, they do not attain a status worthy of separate consideration as a basic element in the box. We are left with questions about how our loyalties affect our ability to consider the facts, and how our choice of a particular mode of reasoning has been influenced by the kind of beliefs in God and human freedom we have accepted as our own. Even more troubling is the lack of a specific reference to our view of society or government and the lack of any discussion of how economic reality—its principles, assumptions, shifts, build-ups, and recessions—affects our fundamental life choices. Further, the box does not elaborate a critical view of society, social change, or culture.

Kammer modifies the Potter Box by elaborating what he takes to be the five most important elements of moralscape. They are ordered hierarchically, the first being the most formative to our decision making, the last the least important in an actual decision. Kammer lists the components: (1) worldview, (2) loyalties, (3) norms and values, (4) experiential and empirical elements, and, lastly, (5) mode of decision making. I visualize Kammer's moralscape as a multilayered circle—the Kammer Circle (see figure 2).

In the Kammer Circle primacy is given to *worldview*. Worldview is the most inclusive framework, those "interpretive processes which are largely products of the societies and communities in which we live, and we are socialized into their views."[3] Taking a strongly relativist position,

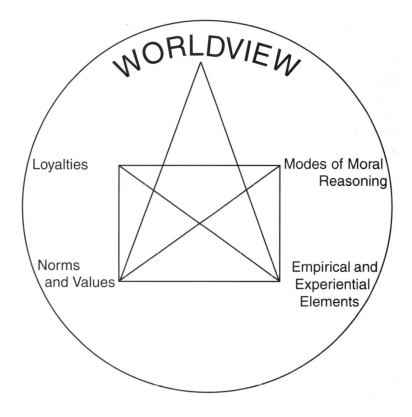

FIGURE 2. THE KAMMER CIRCLE

Kammer believes that one cannot ever prove the ultimate truth or fal-
sity of any particular worldview, yet the adequacy of any worldview can
be assessed and evaluated "by testing its parts for internal consistencies,
or by seeing whether it provides an adequate description of our experience." For Kammer the notion of worldview is more adequate and
comprehensive a concept than Potter's quasi-theological beliefs because it allows for views of individual and society that may exclude reference to God. Further, the concept of worldview allows for general,
largely philosophical presumptions concerning fundamental, underlying
principles and powers affecting nature and history. Worldviews also include presumptions about human nature, the nature of the world, and
society.[4]

Out of the primacy of worldview, Kammer proceeds to define *loy-alties*. He notes that loyalties emerge from the *affective*, while world-views are understood as *cognitive*. Loyalties are the *affective bonds of commitment* in human life. Loyalties are important to Kammer be-cause they present a more expansive view of the human person, not only as rational or contemplative but also as loving, desiring beings. Further, loyalties are multiple, and as such they are the basis of the eth-ical dilemma; loyalties occasionally collide, and deciding which loyalty is more important requires reflection.[5] In a Journey model of ethics, such a definition of loyalties is key to understanding the phenomenon of "dirty hands, holy hands." Our moral hands get dirty because we have been compelled by a particular situation or environment to choose and act in the interest of one loyalty over and against another important loyalty.

The third aspect of the Kammer Circle also grows out of one's world-view: the basic ethical terms *norms* and *values*. The Potter Box assumes that the user understands these terms, whereas Kammer defines the terms and specifies them as an important component in moral rea-soning. *Values* are those things we desire, things that give purpose and direction to our lives. *Norms* are the "rules and guidelines used to in-form our behavior," which we use to attain our values. Stressing the importance of critical reasoning and "self-conscious reflection," Kam-mer encourages us to question the consistency between norms and values and worldview—for example, whether placing high value on so-cial justice squares with the uncritical civic values of national strength and superiority.[6] Such an example reveals Kammer's personal stress on the importance of liberation as an important social-justice value.

The fourth component of the Kammer Circle demonstrates the interrelationship between one's worldview/loyalties/norms/values and the situation at hand. Kammer is not interested in merely accounting for what are taken to be facts, but strives to understand the experiential el-ements that color our ability to interpret which empirical elements are meaningful. Kammer trusts in our ability to modify and correct the limitations of our own experiential frameworks by "ethical reflection" on the experiences of others. Ethical reflection, so cast, relativizes ten-dencies toward universalizing our personal experiences in that it insists that we expose ourselves to other, sometimes conflicting cultural experiences. Why, we might ask Kammer, is it necessary for us to listen to other, unfamiliar cultural experiences? Kammer is attempting to show how concepts of worldview are not frozen or predetermined by our up-bringing or local cultural experiences. Rather, through ethical reflection, careful listening, and a deliberate desire to value the conflicting experiences of other cultures, the moral evils and ethical wrongs of our own cultures can be uncovered, revealed, and potentially liberated.

Modes of moral reasoning are not primary in the Kammer Circle. Reversing the traditional methodological tendency of ethicists to define moral choice according to the mode of moral reasoning employed, Kammer notes instead that one's mode of moral reasoning is not as de-cisive a factor in decision making as are the elements of worldview and loyalties. Notice the familiar way in which Kammer defines the two gen-eral kinds of mode:

1. The *deontological* mode stresses duty, rules, laws, and obligations. Deontologists define a moral action (or decision) as one that conforms to the rules designated.

2. The *teleological* approach is concerned with realizing or embody-ing a sought-after end. Rather than emphasizing duty, as does the de-ontologist, the teleologist is deeply concerned about the consequences of decisions, judging the morality of an act or choice by its capacity "to accomplish a desired end." [7]

Deeply committed to improving the quality of social justice in the world and heartened by what he takes to be the liberating character of pluralism, Kammer constructs his circle in accordance with two guid-ing, fundamental moral questions: "What should we be?" and "What kinds of communities should we build?" [8]

It is important to note how different Kammer's two questions are from what can be gleaned as the fundamental moral questions of Chris-tian fundamentalists, such as Norman Geisler. Although not explicitly stated, Geisler's constructive fundamentalist ethic is motivated by the following questions: "Is it God's will?" and "Is it based on God's revela-tion in the Bible?" [9]

Geisler's fundamental questions are explicitly *theocentric*, or God-centered, while Kammer's guiding questions are *anthropocentric*—concerned primarily with human beings. The differing solutions that eventually flow from these two contrasting views reveal how important the guiding and motivating questions of our moralscape are for addressing ethics. These views have very different starting points, and as a consequence, Kammer's argument moves toward clarifying human concerns, while Geisler's argument struggles to represent a view from God's perspective.

The Journey model of ethics I am seeking to construct embodies something of a middle way (similar to the *via media* of classical theology) between Kammer's concern for nurturing self and community and Geisler's determination to found all moral action within the purview of God, Spirit, and revelation. Middle-way Christians are people who believe in Jesus as the Christ who came into the world, lived as preacher-teacher and healer, died on a cross, rose from the dead, and remains actively present to us in the form of the Holy Spirit; who believe in the Bible as authoritative to the life of faith; who follow, to the best of their finite human abilities, the way as Jesus did in his life; and who live out with equal fervor both the social justice mandates of Matt. 25:31-46 and the individual ethical norms presented in the Sermons on the Mount and Plain (Matt. 5–7 and Luke 6). For a middle-way Christian, the fundamental Christian imperative to follow God's will and hold to the centrality of the Bible cannot be ignored. Furthermore, in agreement with Geisler, middle-way Christians endanger the vitality of our faith if we de-center our theological reflections by rooting our theologies in sociological reality rather than in the ongoing Ultimate that is God as revealed in Jesus the Christ. If we neglect this root of Christian ethics, then we undermine our understanding of God's ability to effectively act through Christ and the Holy Spirit in us as moral agents.[10]

At the same time, the social-justice imperatives suggested in Kammer's two questions about personal and communal integrity are of equal significance. Following the historic precedents of such figures as John Wesley, Harriet Tubman, Walter Rauschenbusch, and Martin Luther King Jr., middle-way Christians hold fast to the progressive social ideals we believe are inherent in the gospel of Jesus Christ. For a middle-way Christian, such questions *must* be held together, lest our faith become fragmented into enervating ideological squabbles. With such squabbling, the rich emulation of Jesus' spiritual holiness is reduced to slavish attention to clichéd doctrinal lists that become lines of demarcation between so-called real Christians and others variously demonized as "sub-Christian" or "neo-pagan." Further, as was suggested in the first chapter, part of the motivation for undertaking a Journey moralscape comes from recognizing that Christians of all sorts and descriptions cannot actually understand our particular moralscape without learning something about its place in the global environment of many religions. Christianity informs and shapes a particular kind of understanding that is based on its fundamental *theocentric*, or God-centered, orientation. Buddhism is not theocentric, nor can it be, because it is not a divinity-centered religion. Although native traditions throughout the world recognize the existence and even the ontological primacy of a Creator or Great Spirit, they are not theocentric either. Rather, they share with great mystical traditions a *pantheism* (God is *in* and *throughout* the entire cosmos), and one might understand them more honestly as being Spirit-centered or creation-centered religions. A middle-way Christian moralscape is captivated by the possibilities of locating itself in the flux and flow of many powerful understandings of religion, not as a cop-out to a demystifying agenda that enervates our faith but as a way of expressing the security of our belief while admitting to its particularity. The Journey model of ethics seeks to build on the positive view of moralscape provided by Kammer, while specifying ways in which the formative theocentric characteristics noted by Geisler can be uplifted as necessary and valuable.

A JOURNEY MORALSCAPE

A Journey moralscape expands and clarifies the components of the most important aspect of the Kammer Circle—the worldview. In particular, a Journey moralscape elaborates the following necessary components of worldview, renaming them moral metaphysics and cultural logics.

Moral metaphysics is the interaction of our *moral being*—what we *are* as moral agents, otherwise known as character—with our *moral doing*—the actual choices and actions we take that embody and reveal to others our character, the *oughts* of our moral decision making. Such attention to both character and moral action presupposes attention to human beings as moral agents, or moral actors. No matter how rich or poor, intelligent or mentally limited, educated or illiterate, all human beings make ethical decisions. Further, human beings are generally held responsible for the consequences of our decisions. To put it more strongly, no matter what our sociocultural or economic circumstance, we are all capable of moral agency, character, and moral action. Bruce Birch and Larry Rasmussen note that *character* refers to those moral elements we often consider internal to the person or group—motives, dispositions, attitudes, intentions, and perceptions.[11] But they also insist that character not be confined to individuals. Moral questions about character have always also been communal: *"What is the good society, or good community, and who is the good person?"*[12] Questions about character lead us to consider *virtue* (taken from the Latin root word *virtus*, meaning "power" or "excellences"). In a Journey moralscape, character encourages an informed understanding of and striving toward those habitual moral practices that embody moral powers and excellences, or virtue. Through character, persons and groups are predisposed toward choosing and acting for the good because it is the good that influences, informs, and enacts itself through their ethical choices. Our ethical choices, to put it more briefly, are informed by *internalized powers,* or *excellences.* Listing my own version of what these internalized powers include could take up an entire book on virtues. However, following in the large footsteps of that great medieval scholastic Thomas Aquinas, suffice it to say that the cultivation of the cardinal virtues of prudence, temperance, justice, and fortitude is enough to fill a reasonably compassionate and full life. But such a life, however filled with cardinal virtues, could not be considered an adequately *Christian* life because the life of a Christian flows from the death and resurrection of Jesus the Christ and requires something more than the cultivation of cardinal virtues. Christians embody a strenuous yet grace-filled ethic that invites us to deeper service in God and ultimately requires an additional infusion of grace gained by the enlivening life-power of the theological or supernatural virtues—faith, hope, and love. For a follower of Jesus the Christ, all concern for social justice—feeding the hungry, clothing the naked, liberating the enslaved, or calling for the enactment of the biblical Jubilee era—is invariably interwoven with a concern to fulfill all of the personal moral injunctions. These personal moral injunctions are embodied in the call to be truthful, gentle, peaceful, self-controlled, and so forth. Taken as a whole, listing both the supernatural and cardinal virtues, we see a recognition of seven powers or seven supreme virtues. These seven powers, interpreted theologically, have everything to do with both the *is* of our moral being and the *oughts* of our moral doings. The aim or *telos* of both our Christian character and our Christian moral decision making should be to harmonize and embody these two aspects so that they are in agreement with each other. Such an ethical goal, while easily stated, requires a lifetime of committed, ongoing work.

A CRITICAL THEORY OF SOCIETY AND CULTURE. To obtain a view of society and culture that will do more than merely reinforce or reinscribe as inevitable some of the very practices and traditions most inimical to human and natural environments, a critical view of society and culture is needed. While such a statement might seem suspicious of or pessimistic about society, there are strong biblical and historical reasons for seeing both society and culture as a fundamental challenge to the life of faith espoused in Scriptures. One cannot read all of the negative references in the New Testament to the world and the flesh without acknowledging that early Christians had an adversarial view of the Hellenistic culture and the Roman Empire they lived in.

Likewise, a Journey moralscape is fundamentally critical of the unconscious daily cultural codes, practices, mores, and customs which together form what might be called the cultural logics of a society. H. Richard Niebuhr's classic treatment of the differing historical reactions of Christianity to culture, *Christ and Culture*, provides different typologies of that interface, and, like Niebuhr, I retain the typology of "Christ transforming culture" as the *telos* of a middle-way Christian critical view of society and culture because such a conception identifies Christ as a central figure for Christians, as I believe he should remain. But the critical view of society and culture espoused in this Journey moralscape owes as much to the school of critical theory as it has developed since the 1930s by Max Horkheimer and Theodor Adorno, and as it is now hotly contested between Jürgen Habermas and Michel Foucault. Further, the poststructuralist theory of practice espoused by Pierre Bourdieu is helpful. Critical theory has much to offer a Journey moralscape because it attempts to provide a view of society and culture that sees human agency as more than just "other-directed authority" (or, to use Niebuhr's term, *heteronomy*). It also transcends modernity's tendency toward individualistic and atomistic ideology (or, to use Niebuhr's term, *autonomy*). At its best, critical theory attempts to "unearth the historical and social genesis of the facts it examines and the social contexts in which its results will have their effects." Critical theorists attempt to locate particular practices and develop a view of culture and society that takes into account the "big pictures and grand narratives as *ongoing accomplishments*" that "are never finished, but *have to be constructed, deconstructed, and reconstructed* [emphasis mine] in ever-changing circumstances."[13] As particularly revealed in the work of Jürgen Habermas, critical theory attempts to combine the research dimension of social science with the critically reflective dimension of philosophy. A Journey moralscape adds to the social scientific and philosophical dimensions a theological basis, which insists that the ultimate goal of a Christian's critical view of society and culture is to demonstrate that a theocentric and/or Christocentric moral *telos* for society and culture is needed to anchor the ongoing construction, deconstruction, and reconstruction of moral meaning. Stated negatively, without a theocentric and/or Christocentric moral *telos,* society and culture can degenerate into moral anarchy, violence, and the dissipation of a sense of a common good. While one could write a book on the interrelationship between morality and critical theory, Craig Calhoun provides us with four key means by which critical theory realizes itself:

1. in a critical engagement with the theorist's contemporary social world, recognizing that the existing state of affairs does not exhaust all possibilities and offering positive implications for social action;

2. in a critical account of the historical and cultural conditions (both social and personal) on which the theorist's own intellectual activity depends;

3. in a continuous critical re-examination of the constitutive categories and conceptual frameworks of the theorist's understanding, including the historical construction of those frameworks; and

4. in a critical confrontation with other works of social explanation that not only establishes their good and bad points, but also shows the reasons for their blind spots and misunderstandings and demonstrates the capacity to incorporate their insights onto stronger foundations.[14]

While critical theory offers a wealth of insights for Christian ethics, our challenge is to identify its most salient and fruitful concepts and incorporate them into the moralscape, the process of ethical discern-ment. Critical theory as a set of ideas and a way of inquiry can help us (1) overcome the modern world's denigration of difference, (2) see the many complex layers of our moral dispositions and actions, and (3) show how social, economic, and political factors figure in all our de-cision making. figure 3 presents what I call the Triangle of Critique, presenting three elements that are necessary if the incorporation of genuinely critical theory of culture and society is to have a potent im-pact on one's ethical journey.

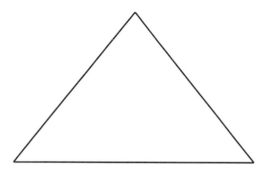

1.Valorizing Cultural Difference

2. Awareness of Habitus, Field, Capital

3. Explicit Awareness of Political and Economic Systems

FIGURE 3. THE TRIANGLE OF CRITIQUE

Valorizing Cultural Difference. Recognizing cultural difference as a positive aspect of one's sociocultural world has been an ongoing prob-lem for the modern West. As critical theory has helped us see, the Cartesian thrust of thought, with its philosophical urge to categorize and define all things in nature, became embedded in various European nations as a moral condemnation of any and all cultural difference. Simply put, "difference is bad" became not only a vague feeling, but the basis for the construction of various hierarchical theories and prac-tices. Perhaps the most notorious of these practices were slavery and colonialism—both being the complete antithesis of the egalitarian political foundation espoused by modern philosophers such as John Locke, François Voltaire, and Jean-Jacques Rousseau. Further, even the egalitarian thinking of Voltaire and Rousseau demonstrated their aversion to cultural difference in such ugly categories as Rousseau's "noble savage."

An adequate critical theory criticizes even influential theorists, such as Habermas himself, for their inattentiveness to this problem and for how such inattention undermines certain key aims of their theory. For example, as Calhoun points out, Habermas's model of *conversation* as an appropriate way of describing sociocultural interaction assumes *one* sociocultural world in which human beings naturally inhabit a single horizon of experience, a single social world, at a time.[15] Calhoun rightly notes that most of us exist in *multiple* and *internally differentiated social worlds*. Many of us live out W. E. B. Du Bois's notion of a *double-consciousness* (for example, Du Bois lived as both an *African* and an *American* at the same time). Conversation does not take place in a power vacuum, where all are simply "accepted" as equal partners in the conversation. As is the case between empowered and disempowered peoples even now, conversation can become the occasion for demonstrating one's sociocultural power over another human being. Extending Calhoun's critique, a Journey moralscape recognizes that one's worldview ought to be constructed in such a way that the *multiplicity* of our cultural contacts, and the *polyphony* of our everyday discourses and conversations are valorized.

Why is this important? Even a cursory examination of how acceptable it is to disparage cultural difference in the United States should set off warning bells for any moralist concerned with developing notions of what a *common good* might be. Much public discussion about difference has taken a decidedly nativistic tone, proclaimed by those champions of so-called conservative, family values who claim that their interpretation of Christianity is the *only* Christian voice. Yet the common good cannot be established if the plurality of our sociocultural reality is not recognized and valorized. Christian conversation ought help Americans embrace difference as we journey toward discovery of a common good. Sensible, middle-way Christians can hold the center, lest it be torn asunder, by becoming more active in public discussions of what a Christian position on these matters might be.

Society's multicultural and globalizing character mean that we inhabit multiple worlds daily. Our coexistence in a medley of sociocultural worlds is particularly clear to those who live in large urban centers such as New York or Los Angeles, where merely walking down the street can be an occasion for multiple cultural contacts. Yet even in rural and agrarian settings, homogeneous and monological cultures are being challenged to find ways to meet and accept others who do not share their language, traditions, and values. Difference is not only "good" but also a simple fact in contemporary life, and so a necessary, constitutive element of our common good.

Awareness of Habitus, Field, and Capital. Habitus, field, and *capital* are three key terms developed by Pierre Bourdieu; they are all useful for deploying critical theory in a Journey moralscape. Bourdieu attempted to understand how human practices are constituted while avoiding the determinism of social-structure theory on the one side (which Bourdieu calls "objectivism"), and overly subjective accounts on the other (or "subjectivism"). He retrieved the traditional scholastic notion of *habitus. Habitus* refers to those "systems of durable, transposable *dispositions*, structured structures predisposed to function as structuring structures."[16] *Habitus* is the source and producer of our practices, inculcated from childhood, that becomes the "generative principle of regulated improvisations" rather than strict imitations of what has gone on before.[17] As such it is a *sense pratique*, or "practical sense," that provides a feel for the game of life choices, that becomes a sixth sense or second nature through the long inculcating process. *Habitus* is that which "inclines agents to act and react in specific situations in a manner that is not always calculated and that is not simply a question of conscious obedience to rule" but is a "set of dispositions." These dispositions are said to be "durable in that they last throughout an agent's lifetime . . . 'transposable' in that they may generate practices in multiple and diverse fields of activity, and are 'structured structures' in that they inevitably incorporate the objective social conditions of their inculcation."[18]

Since agents do not act in a cultural or practical vacuum, Bourdieu developed the concept of *field* (*champ* in French) as a way of theoretically describing structured human activity that is hierarchically organ-

ized, "each defined as a structured space with its own laws of functioning and its own relations of force." Fields are dynamic because
their structure, "at any given moment, is determined by the relations
between the positions agents occupy in the field," so that a positional
shift in the relationship between the agents creates a change in the
field's structure.[19] Bourdieu understands a field to be a *competitive
space* wherein agents compete with each other in an ongoing struggle
to wrest control of the resources and interests that typify their field.
Utilizing the economic metaphor of *capital*, Bourdieu elaborates the
conception of field by describing the inherent competition for resources and interests as a struggle for capital—that is, "the concept of
symbolic power based on diverse forms of capital which are not re-
ducible to economic capital." Capital in the cultural field, for example,
is the result of competition between agents for "the authority inherent
in recognition, consecration, and prestige." *Academic capital*, on the
other hand, is derived from one's "formal education . . . measured by
degrees or diplomas held," while *economic capital* is the resource
derived from the raw competition for control of monetary resources.
Bourdieu is particularly interested in two forms of capital in the field
of cultural production: (1) *symbolic capital*, which "refers to the degree
of accumulated prestige, celebrity, consecration or honour and is
founded on a dialectic of knowledge (*connaissance*) and recognition
(*reconnaissance*); and (2) *cultural capital*, which is concerned with
"forms of cultural knowledge, competencies or dispositions." Because
cultural capital is a form of knowledge, Bourdieu sees it as "an internalized code or a cognitive acquisition that equips the social agent
with empathy towards, appreciation for, or competence in deciphering
cultural relations and cultural artefacts."[20] All of Bourdieu's forms of
capital, as is true for economic capital, are "unequally distributed
among social classes and class fractions,"[21] and therefore are accumulated in a competitive struggle for power and control.

USING CRITICAL THEORY

In a Journey moralscape, we might employ and deploy Bourdieu's
concepts of *habitus*, field, and capital as ways of describing our sociocultural milieu, but it is also necessary to note that his conceptuality

is limited by its economic metaphors. As we deploy critical theory's concepts to help us understand how and why we make the choices we do, we should also realize that describing all of our choices and actions in economic rhetoric may grant a kind of false, materialist shimmer to our words that rings dissonantly against the spiritual claims of faith.

One might well ask, "Why use such ideas, then, if they seem to inherently de-spiritualize our language, and if they appear to reduce the intangibleness of 'culture' and 'symbol' into the gritty materialism of 'capital'?" I believe that Bourdieu's rhetoric is particularly significant and appropriate for persons trying to grapple with the ethical dilemma of dirty hands, for those persons of faith trying to live out the deontological principles received as revelation from the divine. The sociocultural milieu in which most Westerners have been raised—from the poorest to the richest, no matter what subcultural ethnicity, race, or color—has produced a macro-habitus of material desire, the inculcation of a fierce competitiveness to accumulate capital of all forms, resulting in an unforeseen devaluing of human dignity and labor in favor of maximizing monetary profit by any means necessary. Such a statement is necessarily a generalized pronouncement, and many of us might find ways to speak about our own family's micro-*habitus* of loyalty, thrift, and appreciation for the inherent dignity of all labor, humanity, and nature. Yet it is also an indisputable fact that the macro-*habitus* of consumptive, competitive, materialist hedonism has severely restricted the moral vision of *all* Western nations and peoples and constricted our ethical capacities to grapple effectively with global problems of hunger, poverty, and environmental destruction.

Sifting critically through the interaction of our own micro-*habitus* with the dominant macro-*habitus* of our larger sociocultural world is part of the necessary ethical discernment inherent in a Journey moralscape. To put it another way, as we recognize our moral agency as an ongoing journey, we also need to recognize the critical boundaries of acceptance and incorporation of the macro-*habitus* in our ethical reflection, as well as those thoroughly individual or familial dispositions inculcated by our micro-*habitus*. The true usefulness of this aspect of the Journey moralscape is that it can help persons become aware of the intermixture of both our personal experiences, impressions, and family lessons *and* the concrete facts of our social and community contexts.

Why is this important? In many venues for popular discussion in the United States—in the classroom, on television talk shows, radio call-in shows, and so on—we hear persons presenting their opinion forcefully, representing their personal pain, suffering, or affirmations as somehow characteristic and representative of a larger, albeit unquantified group of others "out there who feel just like I do." Such talk is cheap, divisive, and often presented as a part of a general recommendation to "feel good about yourself no matter how sleazy you are." It is representative of an expressive culture that seems incapable of presenting critical reflection but excels in producing reactions. Reaction presents emotional feelings unchecked by reference to facts and lacking consideration of the limitations of one's personal experience. Ethical reflection, on the other hand, insists that our social location and our possible privileges or disadvantages, as well as our emotional reactions, must all be taken into consideration before moral judgments are pronounced as "true" or "good." Ethical reflection insists that "opinion" must take its place in a community context where facts, experiences, and various contested versions of "history" are sorted out, sifted through, and debated. Reflection requires *critical discernment*. Discernment requires reference to and respect for the empirical data and experiences of other persons located in radically different, sometimes conflicting social locations. Ethical reflection says, in a sense, "I am not, and can never be, the measure of all truth, right, and good without a community to check, argue, and confirm my experience."

EXPLICIT AWARENESS OF POLITICAL AND ECONOMIC SYSTEMS. Explicit awareness of the political and economic systems that influence our ideas of the good is also an important contribution from critical theory. Those behaviors and regulated improvisational adjustments that are inherent in our *habitus* are tinged with the specific injunctions, imperatives, and punitive impositions that our political and economic systems have woven into our everyday existence. We can see the variability of these systems by noting how a concept like *rights* functions in different settings. That rich conception known as rights has a complex history that is specific to each context—far different for contemporary persons living in the United States than for persons living in the new South Africa. Fundamentally I define rights as those a priori principles ensured by the government as the secure basis for the exercise of dignity guaranteed to all citizens. To put it another way, rights guarantee a social place or space in which life may be lived. In the United States we have an elaborate Bill of Rights, which secures everything from the right to free speech, the right to an unfettered press, and the right to religious expressions freed from the perils of particularist political and governmental policies, to the right of all persons to vote no matter what their gender, skin color, or creedal affiliation. The original "shorthand" for these political rights came in the threefold proclamation in the Declaration of Independence, that all had the right to "Life, Liberty, and the pursuit of Happiness." The threefold cry of the French Revolution is significantly different—"*Liberté* (liberty), *Fraternité* (brotherhood), *Egalité* (equality)." The former Soviet Union believed that it was the government's responsibility to guarantee all citizens a job, shelter, and equality. The new constitution of South Africa makes guarantees that specifically denounce discrimination based on sexual preference—an innovation that would be a difficult pill to swallow for many freedom-loving Americans, to be sure!

As the movement of a Journey moralscape is *diunital*—that is, inclusive rather than divisive—it becomes necessary for us to sift critically through the strengths and weaknesses of our own particular political evaluation of what constitutes a right and reground our politics in the firmer soil of those biblical imperatives that emphasize social justice, fierce compassion, and activist concern for those who have no social rights or place. Arthur Dyck notes that a reconceptualized view of rights sees them as *just* (fair) *expectations claims*.[22] Moving beyond the prevailing Western individualized traditions (from John Locke and Thomas Hobbes to Alan Gewirth), Dyck reinvigorates a social understanding of rights as justice expressed in a social and communal context that nurtures responsibility.[23] Dyck's reconfiguration of rights has immediate and powerful implications for political and economic theory because it suggests the manner in which social policies ought to be reformulated. Dyck suggests that whatever is decided ought to fulfill the ethical imperative for justice expressed in nurture and responsibility for the community, rather than being merely the insurance of an individual's freedom to pursue self-fulfillment, as often cast in the rhetoric of "rights"[24] in the United States.

SYSTEMATIC THEOLOGICAL ARTICULATION. Returning to our elaboration of the Kammer Circle, we see that systematic theological articulation is suggested there but not elaborated as a key element. Kammer offers a theological framework in a chapter titled "The Sources of Christian Ethics," citing the role and authority of the Bible and the person and teachings of Jesus.[25] Further, Kammer's elaboration of the category "worldview" suggests that a systematic theological articulation could be part of a critical ethic. Kammer accomplishes this by beginning his discussion with an extended look at Christian views of the divine nature, then proceeding to discuss the nature and role of evil, human nature, the natural world, and the nature of society.[26]

The following categories, more fully elaborated in *My Sister, My Brother: Womanist and Xodus God-Talk* (Orbis 1996), provide an outline of how a systematic theology might be constructed to be applicable to our moral decision making.

- God
- World and Evil
- Humanity
- The Problem of Sin
- The Answer in Christ
- Church
- The Authority of Scripture

God. A Journey moralscape that is broadly Christian, or middle-way Christian, expresses its theocentricity by beginning with the concept of God. Of every Christian theology we must ask ourselves, "How does it represent the divine?" God is the ultimate, most meaningful, and most comprehensive term for, as Anselm of Canterbury put it, "that than which nothing greater can be conceived." As a signifier of ultimacy, God relativizes all aspiring claims on our life for absolute and complete devotion. In our capitalist world, where material wealth can be touched, enjoyed, and directly experienced, we Christians say that the God who cannot be touched or directly experienced is nevertheless the most "real" and proper object of our devotion, affection, loyalty, and commitment. Thus, God relativizes and makes idolatrous all of the demi- and semigods of this world, showing them up for the icons of hedonism that they are. God even dethrones the "God" constructed by various doctrinaire versions of Christianity, showing "him" up for the pretender that "he" (as a reified male) is. Substantively, God dethrones all inadequate visions of divinity by being, most simply, the "I am that I am" found in Exodus. In Hebrew this enigmatic phrase combines future, present, and past together so that a more complete translation of God's name would be "I used to be what I used to be, I am what I am, I shall be what I shall be." God *is*, or to put it more forcefully in black English, God *be's*. The God who *be's* everything is the Great *is*, and as such, is God. No created thing on earth or beyond it can claim such ultimacy, no matter how beautiful, wealthy, interesting, or intriguing.

The signal ethical import of God is that from this conception, all other idealisms, faiths, and beliefs are ordered and brought into a kind of numerical valuing. God is, or rather, God ought to be our first loyalty and ultimate concern as moral agents. Put another way, every ethical decision is brought into the compelling ordering authority of God by the question, "Does this choice exemplify the activity of God in my life?" This question holds our ethical attention in a way that no other concept can because it is an idea directed at what is ultimate.

World and Evil. World is the category that challenges simplistic understandings of God because it is the category that describes what the Creator has created. Is God the ultimate moral good? If we say a glib "Yes!" we are faced with the grave problem of how a good and ultimate God could allow evil and sin to exist in the world. If God could prevent evil and does not, then God must either be not entirely "good" or lacking in ultimacy in some sense (be it in power, knowledge, or presence). If we take the conception of God seriously, which all Christians ostensibly do, then the problem of evil, the thorn in our side, quickly arises. This category answers the fundamental question, "If God is Creator in any sense, then why is God's creation not morally perfect?"

My theological construction seeks to find a middle way between the so-called *finite God* of process theology and the *arbitrary God* of traditional Calvinist-influenced evangelical doctrine. If God is ultimate, then neither God's unlimited freedom (the concern of traditionalists) nor the divinity's capacity to transform or mutate with the flow and flux of the cosmos (the concern of process theologians) can adequately capture or fully name the entirety of God. God is both present and absent, and it is out of the mystery of God's absence in our lives that the mystery of evil arises. Evil seems a part of the divine mystery, the negative consequence (not the positive manifestation) of God's absence. Sin, on the other hand, is *our* separation from God. It is a *human-centered* problem.

Such a definition does not satisfy our moral requirements for God to be good. Traditionalists solve this by saying that we human beings have no ontic right to demand that God conform to our limited expectations of what the ultimate good might be. Such an answer subverts and perhaps even precludes our question, and it does not respect humanity's need to experience God's goodness. Process understandings of God, on the other hand, tend to separate God's lovingness and goodness from the notion that God is omnipotent (which process theologians find noxious). God's power, in process eyes, is a power to "do everything that the loving ground of all being can do to express and to communicate and fulfill the society of loving beings."[27] Such a construal of God seems to imply that evil is an absence of God's love. John B. Cobb Jr. uses Whiteheadian rhetoric to affirm that because "every occasion of human experience begins with a given past" and God is "the One Who Calls us beyond all that we have become to what we might be," then God influences all events, is influenced by them, and also "takes up into Godself that whole richness of each experience," opening up the possibility for transmuting "in the divine experience, even the failures, miseries, catastrophes, and calamities of life."[28]

In a Journey moralscape, Cobb's view can be appreciated as notably theocentric, but it fails to provide a rich description of how God concretely transforms and empowers us to overcome calamity, injustice, and misery. In the end, God is becoming and being, first and last, "the same yesterday, today, and forever," while also being ever in flux. If God is truly God, then God must be *process* and *person* . . . and *more!* God is beyond our human metaphors and analogies. Evil seems to be part of the created order that God has fashioned. It is a mystery. Recognizing its existence seems to be a part of a healthy awareness of the ungraspable, the uncontrollability of creation. Natural evils such as hurricanes, tornadoes, and the like damage property and even destroy lives, but they are not sinful. Rather, they are part of a larger cycle of forces that seem to be a part of the flux and flow of nature. Therefore, calling a person "evil" is really a mistake. When we do so, we are really making a judgment on the quality of their ethical choices. Instead we ought to call them "sinful" or "morally wrong." All of this, of course, leads to a discussion of humanity.

Humanity. Along with the category *God, humanity* is one of the central conceptions in a theological ethic. Whether one agrees with my above formulations of God and of world and the problem of evil, methodologically both ought to be considered in constructing one's own moralscape. However, talk about God or evil does not in itself provide us with an adequately grounded conception of human beings; that conception has to be spelled out. The category of humanity answers the question, "How are human beings related to God?" I think it important to retain the primacy of the traditional claim that human beings are created in God's image (Gen. 1:26-27), the revered *imago dei* doctrine, because of the strong ethical claims that flow from such an assertion. Because I am created in God's image, I am expected to have a morally sensitive conscience, which judges, corrects, and affirms the moral choices I make; I am expected to treat other human beings and other created things with intrinsic respect because they are creatures of God, as am I; I am expected to recognize that all human beings share the same Creator as I, and to avoid activities that would diminish recognition of the *imago dei*—in myself and others. Without exaggeration, the doctrine of the *imago dei* remains one of the recurring themes in various contextual and liberationist expressions of Christian faith—from womanist and feminist in the North to Latin American, *minjung*, and *dhalit* in the South—because as persons struggle against various forms of human injustice, their appeals to one another are bolstered by the religious claim that we all are created inherently from the same divine stuff, and that God is reflected (or distorted) in our actions toward one another.

The Problem of Sin. Although we are created in God's image, human beings are not morally flawless. The category of sin answers the question, "Why are the creatures who are God's image not capable of moral perfection?" Human beings "fall short of the mark" (the meaning of the Greek word for *sin*) set by God's moral standards.

We are sinners, not because we are "evil," or intrinsically flawed, but because we are human. Unfortunately sin's force can become so institutionalized, so "normal" and everyday, that human beings created in God's image can habitually and repeatedly choose actions that deface, defame, and distort God's image—in themselves and others. Recent theological developments build on the Social Gospel's social understanding of sin as *institutionalized*, noting that the signal event of the Fall in Genesis 2 may be characterized as a "fall into violence" within human nature.[29] The answer to the problem of sin in our lives, according to Christianity, is not more information, better technology, more wealth, state-ensured jobs, legal access to professional opportunities, or plastic surgery to look more beautiful. Rather, Christians turn to Christ.

The Answer in Christ. A theological system that is in any way explicitly Christian must grapple with Christianity's central figure. It must struggle with the interlocked set of questions, "Who is Christ for moral life?" and "Why, or to what extent, does Christ answer the problem of human sin?" As one builds one's own Journey moralscape, the category of Christ arises initially as a *soteriological turn*, or, in traditional language, as the One who "saves" humanity from the enslaving and crippling effects of sin. Sin's debilitation can be emphasized (overmuch, in my opinion) by strong doctrines of original sin that stress human "depravity," or it can be diminished (again, in the extreme) by so-called Pelagian explanations of human sinfulness as a problem of education and "consciousness raising." Christ offers an answer to this problem by revealing the way of life in the midst of death. Sin causes the power of death, misery, and the forces of antilife to flourish. The life of Jesus and his death and resurrection point to the irrepressible, unstoppable, and irresistible power of God to transform tragedy into triumph. Christ is the answer not because he shed blood to atone for our shame in dishonoring God by being sinners. Such blood-sacrifice atonement theories could be applied to a Journey moralscape by others, but a middle-way Christian voice probably would reconstrue Christ's soteriological significance based on the larger framework of his life, death, and resurrection, rather than simply on his death.

To understand Christ's person we need to analyze and appreciate the specific context of his life. Jesus was a first-century Jew who lived in Palestine under Roman imperial power. Jesus' life was spent grappling with the social and moral implications of living out the *mitzvoth*, or "commandments" of Torah—the central moral imperative of Jewish life. As Christians delve into the subtleties of what it means to be on an ethical Journey, we recognize that, because Jesus was a Jew and not a Christian, the Journey immediately calls us into a radical appreciation of other religions.

At this point, Jesus' import can best be seen in light of three pillars of Jewish moral life as centered in Torah and elaborated in the Talmud—*halakah* or discussions on "purely legal matters," *haggadah* or "nonlegal discussions including such varied matters as medical advice, historical anecdotes, moral exhortations, and folklore," and the *midrash*, which are either sermonic implications derived from the biblical text (*midrash haggadah*) or "the laws we derive from the biblical text (*midrash halakah*)."[30]

When seen in light of Jewish moral and religious life, Jesus' parables and sermons can be appreciated as *midrash haggadah*, and his contentions with various "scribes and Pharisees" as the *midrash halakah* that they likely were. Jesus' teaching, preaching, and wondrous deeds serve no ethical purpose unless we remember that the one who called Lazarus back from death was a wandering Jewish teacher (*rabbi*) acting out of his understandings of the principles of divine love. Poetically, as Jesus resurrected Lazarus from the grave, so even today the life of Jesus as Christ resurrects those considered "dead" by society into new life.

Who is Jesus Christ for us today? The figure of Jesus is currently in the center of a contentious arena. Various influential historical reconstructions and popular depictions of Jesus have been shown to be historically inaccurate or serving of particular group interests. For example, dominant social power is legitimated by painting Jesus as the exemplar of one's own ethnic or racial group, while calling Jesus the savior of *all peoples* suggests that every human being ought to be able to see themselves imaged in depictions of Jesus Christ. These two dynamics must be held together, lest Christ become either a religious symbol legitimating the injustices and miseries perpetrated by the status quo, or a mirror for all that a community or nation or ethnic/racial group wishes to project about itself. As an African American follower of Jesus the Christ, I envision Jesus as black. During a study trip to

South Africa in the summer of 1995, I saw marvelous murals depicting Jesus as a Zulu, garbed in the traditional clothing of a Zulu. Likewise, by extension, it seems perfectly reasonable for Jesus to be depicted as Chinese, or as a Latin American *campesino*. In multicultural settings like the United States, it seems incumbent on Christians, who are in everyday contact with the entire spectrum of human cultural differences, to begin intentional re-envisioning of Christ as *multiply incarnated*, rather than uncritically embracing the "white Christ" of traditional and film portrayals. In the United States we ought to find ways to place brown, red, yellow, and black Christs next to the culturally enshrined white Christ as a way of affirming the incarnation in the lives of all peoples. As "the word made flesh" who "lived among us," Christ is rightly envisioned as African as he is incarnated in Africans, as European as he is incarnated in Europeans, and so forth. The ethical import of such christological insistence is that we undermine the predominant legitimating power of the white Jesus whose apoliticism is a useful tool for sanctifying the wedding of white power with narrow conceptions of "the real" America. On our journey we ought even to find ways to affirm the female Christ or *Christa* as a way of envisioning the incarnation of Jesus in female humanity. For some, affirming the *Christa* remains too radical a christological step, but if Jesus is the embodiment of the divine, or the *Emmanuel* (God with us), then God must be with women as well as men.

Church. The category of *church* finds its place answering the question, "What kinds of communities do we need to live the moral life exemplified in Christ?" The church is the necessary community of those "saved by grace." For some, it is a community of liberators serving the Liberator, for others it is the community of those "called" and "delivered." Still others understand church as a broadly based institution created to provide religious sanctification to the sociopolitical status quo. What we can see from these varied interpretations of *church* is that church is the community of those "called out" (*ecclesia*) by Jesus Christ to serve him, nurture each other, and preserve the moral implications of Jesus' gospel. A central biblical image prodding the church to "go into the world" rather than live apart from it comes from the evangelical command to "Go forth and make disciples of all nations" in Matthew 28. What is this gospel of which Jesus understood himself to be the forerunner, or in African christological terms, the First Ancestor? If one proclaims the gospel, one is not confined to merely "saving souls," although such a task is praiseworthy in a middle-way Christian stance. At least as elaborated by Luke 4:18, gospel seems to resonate with the Hebrew social-justice dictum named Jubilee. In the year of Jubilee, prisoners are set free, debtors are released from their debts, and slaves are released from their servitude. All this is done as a manifestation of "the acceptable year of the Lord." So the gospel is necessarily sociopolitical. It is unreservedly involved with social change. It cannot help but be so. If the church, then, is the community of those living out the implications of the gospel, then it must also be an institution that sees itself on the cutting edge of social justice. It ought to lead with ideas, commitment, and *praxis* (sets of ongoing practices).

The Authority of Scripture. How do the church and individual believers know what God, through Christ, wants us to do? The issue of the authority of Scripture answers the ongoing concern in Christian moral life, "How does the Bible provide guidance for our moral life?" The Bible's authority is a central dividing issue among various kinds and types of Christians. Middle-way Christians are concerned to take the traditions of faith represented in the Bible seriously, as excavated and researched by the historical-critical research of biblical scholars. At the same time, middle-way Christians want to hold on to faith in the overall reliability of Scripture to represent accurately, faithfully, and powerfully the intentions not only of the various human authors of certain books in the Bible, but also of God. We are caught in between the fervor of radical historical critics whose concern for unearthing the most accurate historical picture sometimes relegates questions of faith and theology to a back place—or no place—and the equally passionate ire of traditionalist interpreters. Traditionalists have a zeal for preserving the purported "inerrancy" of the biblical text, condemning all who would even consider a historical-critical approach as embracing heresy. Two commentators helpful for us are Bruce Birch and Larry Rasmussen, who warn against "proof-texting" as a way of using biblical texts to micromanage our morality. At the same time they insist on the reliability of scriptural texts to represent authoritatively to contemporary Christian communities faithful "words" about God. Their investigation suggests that Christians should not uplift the Bible so utterly as to commit the sin of idolizing it—committing *bibliolatry*, as they call it. Rather, we should humbly recognize that the Bible is actually a *library;* it is not a single, fully integrated book. So it should not be surprising that various contradictory messages are sometimes presented in the Bible, because it was written to so many diverse communities over a millennium. For Birch and Rasmussen, the historical-critical approach *enables* rather than *disables* a deeper and richer appreciation of the concrete circumstances that the various authors of the Bible were struggling to address as God's faithful witnesses. Birch and Rasmussen are also able to embrace the hermeneutics of various liberation and feminist norms as appropriate for bringing the messages of the biblical text into direct engagement with crucial issues of our time. As a middle-way Christian, I have tried to employ the biblical text in ways that include both a critically reflective historical norm and an affirmation of the Bible's pre-eminence as authoritative source and guide for Christian moral life.

Along with elements of virtue ethics and critical theory, these theological categories provide a rich and complex view of society, theology, the nature of ethical reflection, and its rationale. This Journey moralscape borrows the rest of Kammer's moralscape without apology, recognizing that each larger aspect of the moralscape—loyalties, norms and values, experiential and empirical data, and modes of moral reasoning—can be understood in a more complete fashion than was originally espoused by Kammer. We have augmented the Kammer Circle, just as he augmented the Potter Box, to render the complexity of the moralscape more accurately. Like the Kammer Circle, the Journey moralscape insists that one's loyalties, values, and norms are far more influential in one's ethical decision making than are the particular modes of moral reasoning one employs. At the same time it is important to recognize that the interaction and interrelatedness of each larger aspect of the Journey moralscape influence and are influenced by one another. An image of the Journey moralscape might look like figure 4.

To specify the content of a Journey moralscape, we need to elaborate a view of love that incorporates justice and power. It continues to be difficult for Christian ethics to grapple with this triad of ethical terms in a

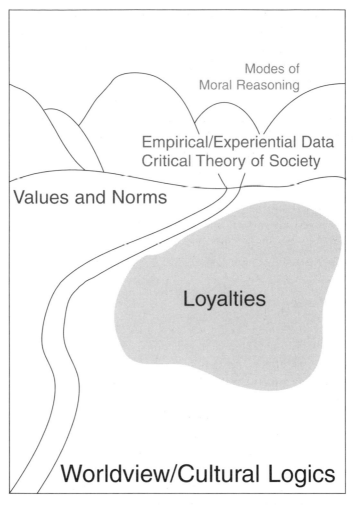

FIGURE 4. A JOURNEY MORALSCAPE

way that empowers our ethical reflections and provides guidance for decision making. We cannot enter the arena of political-economic transformation without understanding how these terms interact in ways that are overlooked or dismissed in general society. Further, when we engage in concrete political and economic reforms that affect those suffering from unjust, unloving power, we need to realize that efforts at maintaining a stance of purported moral purity will inevitably fail and the dirty hands of moral ambiguity will inevitably arise.

FOR FURTHER REFLECTION

1. What would a critical theory of your particular church, political, and social communities look like? How would it compare to the cultural logic of our nation?

2. Practice comparing the moralscapes of two antagonists in current events. For example, in order to understand the reasons behind the Persian Gulf War, one might want to compare and contrast the moralscape of President George Bush with that of Saddam Hussein.

CHAPTER 4

Articulating Love-Justice-Power

Love, in the hands of well-meaning but unaware North American Christians, can become a toxic perversion of God's true *agape*. The Journey model teaches us that those located in a position of global dominance— every person who is a citizen of the United States of America—must apply critical theory's suspicions to themselves in order to be loyal followers of Jesus. The fact is that our everyday practices express dominance of all others around the globe, and when we speak of *love*, it can become the key word for silencing the voices of the poor, a sledgehammer, one more unwelcome demand. Many are the conversations I have heard in which the invocation of "Christian love" only thinly disguised the psychological intent to silence dissent, squelch debate, and stifle difference. I have heard "love" invoked at the most expressive, poignant moments of multicultural debate as a way of precluding conflict in the name of "Christian reconciliation." Such love does not aim toward the sharing of just power through the reconciling grace of God's *agape*. How could love, the ethical centerpiece of typical understandings of the Christian ethos and ethics, *the* supreme value of Christianity, also be something degraded and toxic?

As a follower of Jesus Christ I must ask, "Has love been vitiated by the ambiguities of our dirty hands?" Why such a broad question? Because no one living in the global empire known as "USA" can honestly admit that our hands are not dirtied (here I mean "sullied, implicated") by our pre-eminent global status. Can Christian love, *agape*, be safeguarded from further exploitation? Is it possible for degraded uses of love to become holy again? In this chapter a simple premise is advanced—*When Love is conceived without incorporating an active theory of justice and a realistic critique of power, it is dangerous.* Christian ethics can no longer afford to place a simplified understanding of *agape* as its central theme unless it is willing to find ways of including justice and power as intrinsic to Christian love.

73

What is the interaction of love with justice and power? Love always has a social location and speaks out of certain sociopolitical interests. Love means entirely different things to those who possess culturally legitimated power, the privileges of power over others that the socially empowered possess, than it does to those whose every choice and decision reveal their daily struggle to survive. Distributive justice, the ways in which the goods of a society are distributed and shared, cannot be achieved without some kind of understanding of love, however tacit or assumed. Power, which in its most basic and morally neutral sense means *the capacity to act*, is an ever present adjunct to both love and justice. Without considering the dynamics of power, all Christian discussions of love are anemic and irrelevant and can be used to legitimate dangerous causes. By first considering the classic inadequacies of traditional conceptions of Christian love, I shall move on to discuss how we can recast our politics of love so that justice and power can become intrinsic categories helping us create a more balanced vision of love-justice-power.

WHAT'S LOVE GOT TO DO WITH IT?

We cannot even begin to discuss love without recognizing that love is a complex force of *relationality* in society and culture, far more diverse than our English language affords. For example, in classical Thomistic theology, Aquinas fused Augustine's notion of love with Aristotelian philosophy to speak of *charity (caritas)* as "friendship." But in contemporary parlance, *caritas* has been diminished into *charity*, which connotes the performance of a good deed or set of deeds for persons less fortunate. The relationship has become less important than the act itself.

We are aided if we look at *friendship* as a form of love, as is true in the meaning of its Greek counterpart, *philia*. But how many of us use Greek terms in our everyday language? For Thomas Aquinas *charity (caritas)* is a *divinely infused virtue*, which, along with faith and hope, is God's way of providing a means for supernatural happiness.[1] While charity is a theological or infused virtue, charity for Aquinas is most properly understood as, primarily, friendship of humanity with God, and secondarily, friendship with the creatures that are of God.[2] Friendship, as a form of love in its Aristotelian and Thomistic sense, implies the love of persons who are of equal rank. It is love between brothers and sisters. It is, to use Aquinas's unique language, a form of union with oneself that "goes beyond union with another."[3]

Love is *incarnational*, and as such, love can also be spoken of in both *spiritual* and *physical* terms. Christian ethics has spent many years, many volumes, and much energy describing the spiritual component of God's incarnation through Jesus Christ as a manifestation of God's love. *Agape*, most simply stated, is *God's love*. We shall elaborate the justice and power implications of *agape*, but let us turn first to the more silenced and neglected form of love in Christian ethics. Christians have a difficult time speaking about physical love, be it erotic or sexual. The Greeks called romantic love, love of beauty, and desire *eros*, and the physical expression of love primarily tied to reproduction they called *epithymia*. In today's parlance, *erotic* usually means *sexual*, so contemporary English has blurred two different aspects of love into a mistaken unity.

Paul Tillich broke fresh ground in his brief volume *Love, Power, and Justice* by insisting that there is a continuum of relationship between *epithymia, eros, philia,* and *agape*. Such a connection is almost always downplayed by Christian ethics, which in this respect reflects the West's legacy of negating the body as a symbol of the depth of human spirituality. In Tillich's analysis, *agape* is "the depth of love or love in relation to the ground of life."[4] Yet because love is incarnational, because it seeks to embody itself as it reaches beyond itself, there is a link between sexual love and divine love. In an ontological sense—that is, in the sense that we speak of the *Being* of love—Tillich would say, "All love is one."[5] Although to say this is not heretical, overstressing the point can lead us toward the error of thinking that sexual love and divine love are equal or identical in a moral sense. They are not. We cannot reverse the saying "God is love," because love is not God.[6] Yet *epithymia* is a form of love, sharing in a continuum with *agape* that arises from the ontological unity of all aspects of love. Taking Tillich seriously requires us to engage in radical reconstruction of a Christian view of sexuality. An elaboration of sexual ethics in a Journey moralscape will be articulated in chapter 5.

Tillich's philosophical reformulation of the norm of *agape* in Christianity might be a starting place for relocating love as an immanent power within creation rather than as merely the gift bestowed on a hapless humanity by an utterly transcendent heavenly Father. Love is a power, a power that moves and binds together the universe. It functions analogously to gravity in physics. Yet even though love is a force of attraction and union, it is not something that conforms itself to simplistic descriptions. Love's power seems beyond mere attraction or desire for union. *Agape* is the Christian way of naming that ultimate aspect of love that not only attracts, but also empties itself. *Agape* has a self-empowering, self-enlarging, and self-emptying quality. Yet too much of the Christian theological and ethical tradition has been an extended discourse on *agape* as sacrifice only; such luminaries as Anders Nygren and Karl Barth in the twentieth century have insisted on sacrifice as the exemplification of *agape* in a Christian's life.

LUTHER AND DIRTY HANDS

Anders Nygren's massive and influential tome, *Agape and Eros*, spends several hundred pages in a systematic analysis of *agape* as *the* Christian form of love; subsequently, any form of love that speaks of desire and yearning he judges as sub-Christian. So doing, Nygren condemns Augustine's architectonic treatments of divine love as *caritas*—the yearning and desire of the human soul for union with God. This displacement of Augustine can be understood primarily through Nygren's replacement of Augustinian love ideals with the view of Martin Luther. Luther's emphasis, in Nygren's mind, is solely on what God does *through* humanity. *Agape* is God's work, God's power, and God's gift. Humanity has nothing to offer God and must empty itself in order to become the *tubus* (an "empty tube" or "channel") through which God's love can flow. Further, Nygren places justice in tension with agapic love, noting that justice has to do with *deserts*, that is, reward and punishment, whereas *agape* is concerned with forgiveness and moves in a fashion inimical to humanity's understandings of merit. Nygren's construal of *agape* uplifts divine majesty and the absolute freedom of God's will, but in so doing it devalues human willpower to the point of subverting human dignity. Such a view of humanity de-emphasizes the *imago dei* as the seat of human dignity, which is intrinsic to a middle-way Christian Journey moralscape, and fails to recognize that the value of love is realized by the norm of justice. Since the Journey moralscape constructed in the previous chapter values liberatory strategies and is concerned to develop an adequate view of justice as it pertains to the quest of human freedom, Nygren's view of *agape* seems to represent a woefully inadequate theory of justice. If God's love is unjust, can it be trusted to empower us?

I cite Nygren's usage of Lutheran *agape* as a classic example of the inadequacy of traditional Christian views of divine love. Of course we misrepresent Luther's view of God's *agape* as inherently unjust to human beings unless we go beyond Nygren's usage of Luther's views to Luther himself. Anyone acquainted with the essay *The Freedom of a Christian* will realize that Luther's ethical argumentation struggles mightily to present both God's love and majesty and the paradox of human freedom. For Luther, a Christian lives in two seemingly opposing offices at the same time: "A Christian is a perfectly free lord of all, subject to none. A Christian is a perfectly dutiful servant of all, subject to all."

Luther was driven by the theological recognition that our human "works" (which in the sixteenth century were penitential practices imposed by priests and the papal Curia of the Roman Catholic Church) cannot earn our way to salvation. Yet, as *The Freedom of a Christian* argues, because faith is the gift of God, by recognizing our human helplessness and inability to earn salvation, we can be granted power to become God's children. Faith and faith alone is the sole and sufficient way to salvation for Luther. This principal, known as *sola fide*, provides the basis for Luther to argue the first side of the paradox, namely, that through the rule of faith operating in redeemed humanity, Christians obtain *spiritual power*, the status of *royalty and priesthood*, and a *lofty dignity*.[8] From this inner transformation, for Luther, a Christian's capacity to do good works will logically follow. Citing the saying of Jesus, "A good tree cannot bear bad fruit, nor can a bad tree bear good fruit"(Matt. 7:18), Luther sees acts of service not as salvific, but as the manifestation of God's work within a Christian. Thus is the second statement of the paradox elaborated—*Christians live for others, for all persons, and for their individual selves.* Interestingly enough, Luther cites human need as the fundamental basis upon which Christian service must be based, saying that the "need and advantage of [the] neighbor" is the proper way that "faith is truly active through love (Gal. 5:6)."[9] Here it is clear how Martin Luther sees *agape*: he views it as God's love manifesting itself in our willingness to serve others' needs.

The basis for understanding both a positive view of redeemed human beings and a positive social ethic is articulated in *The Freedom of a Christian*. Luther describes love as non-obligatory and other-concerned. Examining the ordering of 1 Cor. 13:13—"And now faith, hope, and love abide, these three, and the greatest of these is love,"— Luther sees faith as primary, or at least as first in the order of time, in the progression of the virtues bestowed by God. From faith, according to Luther, flows "love and joy in the Lord," and likewise, "from love a joyful, willing, and free mind that serves one's neighbor willingly and takes no account of gratitude or ingratitude, of praise or blame, of gain or loss."[10]

At the same, however, applying a critical social-theory methodology (an intrinsic part of a Journey moralscape) to Luther's affirmation reveals some troubling applications. Luther's love concept is embodied in dirty hands when he weds this other-concerned, non-obligatory *praxis* to a strictly literal interpretation of the Pauline injunction to "be subject" to temporal governments. How does one subject one's self to the violent and occasionally genocidal policies of a temporal government as a Christian? "Dirty hands" here implies the moral ambiguity of positive law abiding in conflict with possibly "higher" forms of Christian pacifism and *agape*. Luther more fully elaborates his two-kingdom moral stance in a later treatise, *Temporal Authority: To What Extent It Should Be Obeyed*. However, in *The Freedom of a Christian* we find the telling indication of his refusal to criticize radically temporal injustice or institutions/persons/authorities in government. Luther exhorts his readers to subject themselves to service and to government authorities, not to justify themselves, "since they are already righteous through faith, but that in the liberty of the Spirit they shall by so doing [subjecting themselves] serve others and the authorities and obey their will freely and out of love."[11] If we read this carefully, we see that Luther is actually conflating subjection and obedience with love and service. Restated, Luther's dictum here might be:

Because one is utterly free in the Lord, and through faith has been given the freedom of God's *agape*, then a Christian ought to reveal that gift of love by utterly serving the needs of all, obeying and being subject to all government authorities.

As might be suspected, such a casting of *agape* makes it a ripe candidate as a tool for exploiting the poor and manipulating the weak. From a critical feminist/womanist point of view, such an ethic gives religious legitimation to the abuse of women and children. Also, because this view does not specify what the need of my neighbor might be, it could be used as a way for others to manipulate me, rather than as an opening for my service to others. My neighbor might decree any number of things as a dire need demanding a Christian response, and in my attempt to satisfy these needs I might deplete my own resources, burn out my energy reserves, and spiral into self-abnegation. Luther has very little trust in the self, or "the heart," and so he has very little interest in examining how time, energy, and *agape* ought to be directed toward oneself. By constructing *agape* as solely directed outward to others, Luther's vision suffers from an enervation of self-love. By focusing on the supremacy of God's grace and the primacy of faith, Luther's definition of *agape* unintentionally can lead to a denigrated and undignified believer, saved by grace, and damned to a hellish temporal existence of obedience, subjection, and oppressive servitude.

The dirty hands ambiguity in Luther's understanding of love, justice, and the power of temporal governments is even more clearly revealed in his *Temporal Authority: To What Extent It Should Be Obeyed*. Since Luther had been sheltered from the ire and power of the Roman Catholic Church by German princes, who had even saved his life upon occasion, he respected the secular powers-that-be as part of God's political design and ethical intention for the world. At the same time, he struggled with the implications of various Scriptures (Matt. 5:38-41; Rom. 12:19,; and 2 Pet. 2:3-9) that counsel nonresistance to evil, love of one's enemies, prayers for one's persecutors, and an attitude that leaves vengeance to God and God alone. Luther struggled with these Scriptures. Eventually some of Luther's preaching and writings would incite the spirit that led to the Peasant's Revolt of 1524–1526 against the injustices of the landowning princes. After the rampage, pillage, and even rape that accompanied the revolt, the princes put down the revolt with violence. Like the peasants, the nobility found comfort in Luther's advice to them, especially in his interpretations of Rom. 13:1-7 in *An Open Letter to the Christian Nobility* (1520) and his violent rejoinder against the rebellious peasants, *Against the Robbing and Murdering Hordes of Peasants* (1525). Luther's advice had been used by both sides! As was no doubt inevitable, both sides eventually believed that Luther had betrayed their side in some sense, and by 1526 his books were being burned in many quarters.

Luther's treatise on *Temporal Authority* was written in 1523 as a way of holding together the tension between obedience and transformation. On the one hand he faced the scriptural injunction to "be subject to the governing authorities," and on the other, the desire for justice among those who suffered oppression under unjust rule. Given the need for obedience, how can Christians rightly go about changing unjust temporal authority? Luther's dilemma is a classic tale of Christian dirty hands, and his "answers" are not only discomforting but, for many of us, wholly inadequate.

For Luther, humanity is divided between two kingdoms—the kingdom of God, and the kingdom of the world. In the kingdom of God, "true believers who are in Christ and under Christ" live under the "lordship" of Christ because for them Christ is both "king" and "Lord."[12] Those whose ethical choices and lifestyles are determined by their life "in and under Christ" have no need for the temporal law or sword, since there would be no need for either in such a life. Luther is certain that true believers fulfill all of the law and more, because under the guidance of the Holy Spirit, they would not participate in injustice, would be loving to all, and would suffer "injustice and even death willingly and cheerfully at the hands of anyone."[13] So in Luther's spiritual kingdom, the Christian embodies a high view of self-sacrifice as a way of expressing love.

The costliness of genuinely living out Luther's rigorous understanding of self-sacrifice leads him to believe that there are not many persons who can live in the spiritual kingdom because, in fact, there are "few true believers and still fewer who live a Christian life."[14] Most people, whether they espouse Christian beliefs or not, function as inhabitants of the kingdom of the world insofar as their concrete ethical choices are concerned. Since most people actually inhabit the secular kingdom, Luther describes it as controlled by sinfulness, wickedness, and injustice, concluding that the temporal sword of force is necessary to restrain the savagery and wild impulses of sin. Force is the regulating norm of the temporal sword. In reality, Luther sees both kingdoms, or "governments," existing side by side. The kingdom of the world needs the moderating influence of the "spiritual sword" working in league with the restraining violence of force. Luther disagrees with the radical reformers (like Ulrich Zwingli) who believed that the world ought to be ruled solely by the gospel rule of love. For Luther, the "rule of the gospel" cannot function as the sole authority for both kingdoms, since a sudden outbreak of wickedness and violence would occur without the balancing restraining force provided by the temporal sword. Further, Luther believes that it is a good thing for Christians to submit willingly to the temporal sword by paying taxes, honoring authorities, serving and assisting in government, and aiding in any and all ways.[15] Christians may serve in government and even as soldiers, not because it benefits them, but "for the sake of others, that they may be protected and that the wicked may not become worse."[16] Sacrificing Christian self-interest, Luther's understanding of Christian love as self sacrifice allows Christians to see themselves as members of the kingdom of God while functioning as Christians ought to in the kingdom of the world.

The metaphor of *kingdom* in Luther may be understood as his extension of the Pauline "flesh" and "Spirit" dichotomy and Augustine's two cities—"the city of Man" and "the city of God." Derived from a Pauline understanding of ethical choice, all of these texts make a clear demarcation for determining what is right and what is wrong for Christians. Not considering the ongoing dilemma of dirty hands, this tradition states that there are two clear moral choices for Christians—either one is deciding something "in Christ" and under the guidance of the Holy Spirit, or one is being led by the various impulses of "the flesh." Luther's innovation is that he tries to show that while our "hearts and spirits" belong to God in God's kingdom, nevertheless our bodies exist under the authority of the temporal sword. Thus, Christians are called to serve God inwardly and to serve the world outwardly.[17] Instead of suggesting that Christians live two separate and distinct lives, Luther seeks to harmonize the overlapping of the two kingdoms by

reconceiving Christian participation in the temporal kingdom as or-
dained by God. Such a course is ethically dangerous, of course, because
it is always difficult to separate one's individual desires and willfulness
(maybe even "will to power") from the scriptural mandates of *agape* and
justice.

Does Luther recommend that Christians follow an unjust or evil
prince? In *Temporal Authority* Luther fudges. On the one hand, he cat-
egorically states, "No, for it is no one's duty to do wrong." Yet, on the
other hand, if it is not clear whether the prince (symbolizing ruling authorities) is right or wrong, Luther falls back on the submission and obedience claims of Romans 13, noting that all that matters is that our conscience be clear before God.[18] Of course, doing what the temporal
authorities demand, even shedding blood unjustly as long as it is done
with a "clear conscience," can be easily refuted by countless examples,
the Nazi horror of exterminating Jews in the Shoah of World War II
being a recent example. We cannot avoid the pain of moral ambiguity
and the "stain" of dirty hands by facile appeals to God's mercy and anemic exhortations to follow orders with a clear conscience.

The bulk of Luther's most controversial claims on the issue of submission or rebellion, however, may be found in another later treatise,
Whether Soldiers, Too, Can Be Saved (1526). Here he takes up these issues more fervently, stating that "our bodies and property are subject to
worldly rulers," and that Christians "owe obedience to worldly rulers."[19]
Christ's "government" is a spiritual government of the heart; if worldly
rulers demand that Christians take up weapons and fight, we must fight!
After the Peasant's Revolt, Luther was highly suspicious of rebellion. He
saw rebellion as fundamentally unjust because it functions to promote
the destruction of "God's ordinance [to submit to the authorities in Romans 13]."[20] He advances the dubious claim that it is God's will for
human beings to endure tyranny or flee from it to another region. Only
on account of insanity could a ruler be rightfully deposed or "put under
restraint." For Luther a "raving tyrant" is not insane but still has the
mental faculties to be persuaded of his wrongdoings and might even be
transformed.[21]

Under the lens of a critical and concrete theory of society and culture within a Journey moralscape, such advice is to be rejected. Ex-
cusing the brutality of tyrants because they still *may* have a conscience

cannot be forwarded in any way as grounds for delaying their removal from governance; the fact remains that they are breaking the formative laws of Torah: "Thou shalt not murder," "Thou shalt not steal," and many times "Thou shalt not covet." Even though life is rife with the tensions of moral ambiguity and with the hesitation that results from trying to do good even when there are evil consequences (the principle of double effect, discussed below), murder, stealing, rape, and the various other measures for social control and dominance used by tyrants ought never to be excused or legitimated by Christian ethical counsel. Luther's counsel was indeed dirty because he owed his very life to the same princes and lords who had brutally slaughtered thousands of peasants in their attempt to restore order. Luther tried to deflect his individual moral dilemma—that of trying to critique the unjust use of princely authority and still criticize the peasants enough to remain in the prince's favor—by reminding the rulers that they could not rest easy in their violent tyranny. Since God is the final preserver of all rulers, Luther reminds the princes that it is God who ultimately appoints and deposes. Further, Luther attempts to comfort the peasants with the threat of God's punishment of tyranny through the invasion of foreign rulers. Genuinely trusting in God's providential nature, Luther notes that God can raise up rulers from other countries, thus allowing "vengeance, punishment, and danger" to hang over the heads of unjust rulers. Such a God, in Luther's mind, acts in a omnipresent fashion: "He is right behind them [unjust rulers]; indeed, he surrounds them and has them between spurs and under bridle."[22] Such counsel, while notable, is so brief in the context of the entire treatise that one might see it as ineffectual against the much more vociferous and long-winded theological harangue against rebellion.

How do we balance the needs of justice in the social realm with the Christian claim of *agape* as fundamentally all-giving, sacrificial, and forgiving? Is it possible for *agape* to be meaningful in society as a spur toward social change, or is the most effective arena for *agape* that of personal ethics and individual responsibility? Such questions are answered in a Journey moralscape by looking at the historical development of the idea of love-justice-power.

JUSTICE

Political theory depends on an understanding of justice, of how the goods of society are both distributed and contribute to the common good, wealth, and health of all peoples. In the contemporary United States, social opinion is fissured when it comes to deciding how the social ideal of caring for all people in tangible ways (which grew from the New Deal policies of Franklin D. Roosevelt as well as various Social Gospel movements in the twentieth century) can be realized in an era of vast economic globalization and the transformation of economic structures. The so-called conservative political response to this dilemma has been to negate the New Deal and Great Society social idealism as a "failed liberal social experiment." Yet the kind of spartan reductions that radical Republican conservatives call for seem to grate against the biblical politicism that has provided a religious legitimation of so-called liberal policies. At a time of such confusion and indecision, public opinion can be easily manipulated by base appeals to nativism, thinly veiled racism, and various other vote-grabbing strategies—all of which serve to further divide rather than unite the body politic. It is the duty of a Journey moralscape to help demonstrate how one's view of justice informs both one's political ideals and one's economic practices.

There are certain descriptive maxims in ethical theory that can provide great clarity in political discussion. One of the best maxims from ethical theory for elaborating how dirty hands and moral ambiguity are fundamental to all political movements is the principle of *double effect*. In essence, the principle of double effect states in abstract terms what having dirty hands is all about—*for every choice and action there is both a positive and a negative consequence or outcome*.

An excellent and well-known example of this principle (although it is usually never described in this way by either side of the argument) is the deployment of so-called affirmative action policies in schools and in the workplace. Countering long-standing traditions of privileged access for European Americans to certain schools and jobs, affirmative action policies originally intended to ensure the consideration of African American people, of women, and of various other disempowered groups for educational and employment openings. Various strategies for achieving greater racial and gender representation in the ranks resulted in the imposition of the now infamous quota system as a way of measuring the success or failure of the program's implementation. Most race-based quotas have never even been achieved, at the workplace or in schools. Nevertheless, from the 1978 Supreme Court case *Bakke vs. Board of Regents* onward, the majority population has increasingly understood affirmative action as equal to "reverse discrimination" against European Americans in general, and white males in particular.

Without a doubt, affirmative action policies have achieved measurable success for some African Americans. The percentage of blacks in the middle class in 1960 was a mere 6 percent, but after some twenty-five years of affirmative action policies, that had risen to almost 33 percent in the 1990 census. At the same time, through a powerful conservative political campaign, most white Americans believe that their interests and their children are hurt by such policies. While the Equal Employment Opportunity Commission (EEOC) reports that only 3 percent of its cases of workplace discrimination involve white males, political and media attention seem to suggest a much greater harm. Obviously, affirmative action policies have resulted in a measurable but limited good, increasing the overall wealth of one-third of the African American community. It has also provided ammunition to those who portray even slight harm against an individual European American as injurious to the whole of America. Blacks in so-called affirmative action positions suffer from an increased lack of respect, are not taken seriously, and experience overt white hostility. So while access has increased (a good), resentment and the fires of overt racism once again have been ignited (a negative or wrong). Such is the principle of double effect, and remedying such social problems requires political solutions that bring people together rather than push them apart. Few discussions have brought whites and blacks together on this issue; rather, most serve to further divide.

A Journey moralscape suggests that in addition to understanding various forms of justice one ought to also continue to note (as did Reinhold Niebuhr, Paul Tillich, and Martin Luther King Jr.) that love, power, and justice operate together. One cannot impose a system of justice (e.g., affirmative action policies as a form of *redistributive justice*). The imposition of any system of redistributive justice in the United States must be accompanied by measures for redressing the power dynamics of predominant European American male dominance in the highest positions. As a form of Christian ethics, a Journey moralscape conception of justice and power necessarily factors in *agape*, for love has the greatest spiritual potential for transforming the persons who practice injustice. We cannot undermine injustice without love-power-justice, for the three operating together preclude any need for numerical quotas—the motivation being to include all persons in economic and political contexts. Why? Such an assertion is based on an understanding of love-power-justice that is *transformative* and *inclusive*.

Karen Lebacqz's *Six Theories of Justice* suggests that there are at least six distinctive traditions of justice:

1. *Utilitarian justice,* the name given "to those rules that protect claims considered essential to the well-being of society . . . subject to the dictates of the greatest good for the greatest number."[23]

2. *Contractarian* justice, as espoused in John Rawls's challenge to utilitarianism, stating most simply that "justice is fairness" because choices are not to be based on their utility but made "by rational choice in a fair setting."[24]

3. *Entitlement or commutative* justice, as espoused in Robert Nozick's critique of John Rawls's ideals. Justice is viewed here as *fairness in exchange*, not measured in substantive claims, but in procedural requirements.[25]

4. *Roman Catholic social encyclicals* or *human dignity* justice, espoused by papal decrees, roots justice not in "societal consensus nor in rational deduction or calculation" but in faith in God and "God's intentions for human life." The impact on human dignity is the fundamental criterion of such a view of justice.[26]

5. *Christian realism* is the Protestant alternative to the Roman Catholic view of justice Lebacqz has chosen. Justice is relational, in dialectical tension with love, which functions as "a cautionary device" and "a principle of prophetic criticism of *any* stance taken." Ever aware of the persistence of sin and human limitation, a realist version of sin serves to goad persons toward a greater approximation of love in society, but justice is never finished or completely achieved.[27]

6. *Liberationist justice,* as developed by Latin American theologian José Porfirio Miranda, states that "justice is not a norm or law, but the establishment and maintenance of right relationships or "righteous-

ness." For the liberationist, justice is not a theory but a radical practice performed, something done, especially in relationship to the victims of injustice—the poor.[28]

In the end we need to find ways to affirm the strengths of each vision of justice, finding ways to incorporate their claims on our constructive ideals of justice. A Journey moralscape suggests that such an incorporative view of justice moves beyond the restrictions of the six traditions listed above, motivated by the contributive ideal. *Contributive justice* holds that our finest and best way to realize fairness and equity and to affirm the dignity of humanity and creation is to participate genuinely in the contribution of our strengths to the common good of our communities. Even in the vile marketplace of bottom-line capitalist competition, there is still room for persons to contribute goods to the welfare of our communities. Of course, wider and narrower versions of "community" are espoused by various political theories. "Local community" takes on greater importance in many conservative political speeches, while intentional commentary on the "global community" has become the province of so-called liberal progressives. It is possible that the local and the global are two poles on a continuum, in creative tension with each other. Perhaps we require strong emphasis from both aspects of community in order to understand the nature of community in its fullest sense. Yet I insist that a contributive ideal of justice needs to become the key element toward a fuller sense of political and economic justice.

POWER

Power, most simply defined, is the capacity or ability to perform an action. As persons living in the United States of America, we tend to associate the word *power* with *politics* and to speak of power as a form of domination, manipulation, and control over people, groups, and things. Thus, power in our contemporary society has become synonymous with a pervasive mood of cynicism and skepticism toward those who speak and act as if they have the ability to transform government, economics, and the political scene in general.

Starhawk, a noted feminist, has provided perhaps one of the most helpful analyses of power. In her book, *Truth or Dare: Encounters with*

Power, Authority, and Mystery, she develops a threefold typology of power: (1) *power-over*, or the power to control and dominate; (2) *power-from-within*, which she links "to the mysteries that awaken our deepest abilities and potential," or *empowerment;* and (3) *power-with*, which is the *social power* exercised in the medium of exchange, respect, and activity between and among equals.[29] Arguing against the pervasive dangers of power-over practices, Starhawk promotes the notions of power-from-within and power-with as necessary for liberative ethics and spirituality.

Although Starhawk is a practitioner of Wicca, a nature religion originating in Old Europe, her insights have a very dynamic application to a middle-way Christian Journey moralscape. Power, as exercised by the God whose most important other name (ethically speaking) is Love (1 John 4:16), is not the activity of a divinity who coerces, controls, manipulates, or dominates to have "his" way. Such an exercise of power is unjust because it does not share the dynamism of *exousia* (one Greek word for *power* meaning authority) or *dunamis* (the other Greek word translated as *power* in the Bible, meaning dynamic energy). As true power is just because it adequately, fairly, and compassionately contributes and distributes itself, so true power is also synonymous with the God whose essence and moral activity is love. True love *empowers*, that is, it enables us to be *more than we were before we encountered it*. True love occurs in the event of *power-with*, in the activity of sharing, contributing, struggling, negotiating, and resolving.

MARTIN LUTHER KING'S SYNTHESIS OF LOVE-POWER-JUSTICE

The theological ethics developed by Martin Luther King Jr. during the heat of protest for greater civil rights provides a Journey moralscape with an excellent example of how Christian ethics can be revised to incorporate love with power and justice. King's understanding of love-power-justice was a creative blend of the activism of his pastoral forebears in the black baptist church with Walter Rauschenbusch's emphasis on the Beloved Community, Anders Nygren's systematic notion of *agape*, and his own work as a nonviolent resister. King came from a long genealogy of preachers, his grandfather and father having distinguished themselves as activists for the black community in Atlanta. His grandfather, A. D. Williams, had been a charter member of the NAACP of Atlanta and had led economic boycotts in the early decades of the twentieth century. His father, affectionately known as "Daddy King" in later years, was renowned for his fierce distaste of the Jim Crow segregation policies of the South and had led economic boycotts in the mid-1940s.

Martin Luther King Jr. grew up in a home where his mother, Alberta Williams King, stressed the duty and obligation of all Christians to love everybody—even racist whites. His father, on the other hand, chafed bitterly against racist practices. He encouraged his son to "stand up" to the "system" that degraded the humanity of African Americans. One could say that this was the groundwork for the mature King's dialectical view of love and justice. Young Martin struggled mightily to hold together in one piece his mother's ethical imperative—love all people, even those whose actions are heinous—with his father's enacted practice of justice, "standing up" to racism whenever he could.

At Crozer Seminary, young Martin learned about Rauschenbusch's vision of love and justice. For Rauschenbusch, the "kingdom of God" is the central symbol and *telos* of Christian life. He defines the kingdom of God as "the organized fellowship of humanity acting under the impulse of love," the "true human community," the "righteous community." Rauschenbusch's work introduced King to the concept for which he was to become an advocate—*the Beloved Community.* In Rauschenbusch's terms, the kingdom of God is "realized" in such a Beloved Community because love is a progressively realized and imparted form of society that expresses itself as service to others. Love is the "supreme law of Christ" and the "society-making quality."[30] Most importantly, King read of Rauschenbusch's insistence that love is an "energy of the will bent on creating fellowship."[31] King was to incorporate this ideal into his freedom struggle.

The work of Anders Nygren was particularly significant for King because it reinforced in his thought some of the foundational teachings he had received about Christian love from his mother and from preaching in the black church. Nygren notes that *agape* is "spontaneous and unmotivated," thus different from the "calculating" and "interested" character of "eros." Further, Nygren believed that *agape* is "indifferent to value," or more clearly, makes "no distinction between the worthy and the unworthy." *Agape* is "creative love" as well; it is "forgiving"; and finally, *agape* is "the initiator of fellowship with God" by God's own volition and creativity.[32]

King interpreted his first battle with segregation as regulated by the norm of love. In *Stride toward Freedom*, King conveyed a systematic viewpoint about *agape* that combines Rauschenbusch, Nygren, and his black church social-activist teachings into a powerful demand for social justice. He insisted that *agape* was the motivating and guiding principle of love that undergirded nonviolent resistance to segregation policies. In King's view, *agape* can be described in this way:

- *Agape* is not the "nonsense" of urging persons to "love their oppressors in the affectionate sense." King was concerned that his mention of "love" would be misunderstood as a passive and foolish sentimentality. For King such a view fundamentally misrepresented the confrontational energy of *agape* when utilized in social-justice activism.
- *Agape* requires "understanding, redemptive good will" for all people, including one's oppressors.
- *Agape* is "overflowing, spontaneous, unmotivated, and groundless." Here King echoed Nygren.
- *Agape* "springs from the need of the other person." Here King insisted that African Americans in the freedom struggle recognize the "need" of white segregationists for the "love of the Negro" in healing their collective, "greatly distorted," and "scarred" personality.
- *Agape* is "disinterested." Thereby neighbors are loved in and for themselves as "children of God."
- *Agape* is "active, community-seeking, [and] community preserving" in its energetic determination.
- *Agape* expresses a "willingness to forgive," which for King meant that black Americans remained open to forgiving whites of "past sins."
- *Agape* "recognizes that all life is interrelated." This means that all humanity (and we would now add, all of creation) is involved in a "single process" of kinship.
- *Agape* is "based on the conviction that the Universe is on the side of justice." This is not only a notion of a cosmic moral law but also

a notion about the theological cosmological roots of justice. King noted that the practitioner of nonviolent *agape* has a "belief in the existence of some creative force that works for universal wholeness." Strengthened by such a belief, the nonviolent resister "knows that in his struggle for justice he has cosmic companionship."[33] For King, this "creative force" was a "personal God," but he cast his reinterpretation of *agape* in wider terms than those of traditional Christianity. A Journey moralscape conception of love-power-justice sees the wisdom of such a broad view. In a middle-way conception, one needs to look toward a multiplicity of cosmic-theological metaphors to describe God's moral activity.

King's view of justice was rooted in a Boston Personalist code of justice that promotes "human personality." In his famous "Letter from Birmingham Jail," King described his vision of justice in relationship to law by answering the question about the freedom struggle's means of "breaking the law." He noted that there were two kinds of law, *just* and *unjust*. He defined a just law as "a man-made code that squares with the moral law or the law of God." The unjust law, in contrast, "is a code that is out of harmony with the moral law." Quoting both Augustine and Thomas Aquinas, King said that such a law is "no law at all."[34] King believed that in being willing to go to jail for breaking an unjust law, one demonstrates the deepest respect for law. What kind of law did King mean? He was talking about a law that was *theocentric* and *deontological*. Further, like the "eternal law" of Aquinas, King's understanding of law provides a metaphysical background for what is "good" and "bad," "just" and "unjust."

King defined *power* very simply in *Where Do We Go from Here: Chaos or Community?* as the "ability to achieve purpose . . . , the strength required to bring about social, political, and economic changes."[35] In this definition, he provided a criticism of various understandings of Black Power in the 1960s that arose from disappointment in the slow pace of racial justice and from the despairing sense that equity would never be achieved in the United States. King believed that the slogan "Black Power!" was essentially an emotional concept without content or political substance. He sought to provide a "broad and positive meaning" to *Black Power* by grounding it in the "demands of love and justice." For King, the traditional practice of contrasting love with power was a deceptive practice because *power is necessary to the most just realization of love*. "What is needed is a realization that power without love is reckless and abusive and that love without power is sentimental and anemic."[36]

For King, power is best understood as "love implementing the demands of justice." Power, then, is the means whereby the energy of love, infused with the concrete demands of justice, acts and accomplishes good in the world. It is a dependent term, neutral in its own ethical valence but prone to recklessness and abuse if not imbued with the strictures of justice. Power requires justice in King's thought. In fact, in the same paragraph in which King defines *power* as love implementing the demands of justice, he added the following definition of *justice*: "Justice at its best is love correcting everything that stands against love."[37]

In a Journey moralscape, love, power, and justice necessarily form a complex yet intimately relational concept. The three inhere, completing and qualifying each other. King's recasting of the word *love* to include justice and power enables us to think of love outside of its sentimental, emotional, and individualized meanings. As recast by Martin Luther King, *love* can mean the powerful willing-toward-community that is necessary if diverse (and often conflicting) peoples are to seek the common good, guided by the imperatives of justice as it works its way in power.

FOR FURTHER REFLECTION

1. To flesh out a view of how Christians relate love to theories of justice and power, try to sketch a Journey moralscape around the central ethical theme of one or more of the following authors: What are the strengths and weakness?[38]
- Walter Rauschenbusch's Progressive Just-Love
- Reinhold Niebuhr's Dialectics of Justice
- Martin Luther King's Somebodyness
- Beverly W. Harrison's Angry Love-Justice
- Emilie Towne's Unctuous Womanist Justice

2. In what ways would you build on your author's insights?

3. Comparing your author's view with those fleshed out by other students, which author's views are closest to your own? Which is furthest from your view of the relationship between love, power, and justice?

4. How would you handle the problem of "dirty hands" tackled by Martin Luther? Do you agree with his analysis? How would your conception of the ways in which Christians participate in "worldly" things differ from his?

CHAPTER 5

Balancing Dirty Hands with Holiness:
A Case Study

The following case study provides an example of how Christians can find themselves caught between the desire to live holy lives and a commitment to actions that may be fraught with ambiguity. The case involves two married ministers, a man and a woman, whose close working ties compelled them to explore issues of the appropriate boundaries of intimacy. We will then use this case to extend the "dirty hands, holy hands" paradigm into the sociopolitical realm of sexual ethics.

INTIMATE BOUNDARIES

John Davis and June Taylor are copastors of the Holy Spirit United Methodist Church of Sedona, Arizona. Both are happily married, John to Rita for twelve years, and June to Jerry for eighteen years. The Davises have three children and the Taylors have five. John and June first got to know one another as students in seminary, and they have both developed strong reputations for planting churches. Each started three churches in the eight years between graduating from seminary and moving to Sedona. Both John and June have built reputations for solid pastoral care, exciting preaching, and belief in the miraculous power of the Holy Spirit. All of the churches they started grew from a handful of people to vibrant flocks of two to three hundred souls within the first year! Because they had both demonstrated such extraordinary gifts of ministry, and wanting to make a strong showing for the gospel of Jesus Christ in an area of great spiritual contention, the bishop assigned them to copastor a new church in the "New Age capital of the Southwest," Sedona, Arizona. Famous for its fantastic rock formations and desert beauty, Sedona has an international reputation as one of the psychic "power points" of the world. It attracts thousands of New Age pilgrims in search of paranormal phenomena and spiritual experiences.

John and June started their Holy Spirit Church with only six persons, with worship in an exceptional lovely spot outside town. So inspiring was their preaching and so meaningful was their care that within a year the small group of followers grew into a regular gathering of three hundred believers. Holy Spirit U.M.C. thrived as a non-traditional "old-stream" church. While they continued to meet outside, eventually they had members who were wealthy enough to erect a beautiful circular edifice in which they could engage in a more institutionalized form of ministry. Holy Spirit had an active outreach ministry to the Navajo Indians who lived nearby, providing detoxification services as well as employment counseling. While most of the members of the church were upper-middle to upper-class European Americans, the church had a 30 percent minority of Mexican Americans and Native Americans and about a 5 percent African American membership. The spiritualities of Hopi, Mayan, Azteca, Navajo, and West African peoples were honored alongside traditional Euro-American worship practices. Things were going very well.

The members of Holy Spirit required a great deal of personal pastoral care. John and June found themselves undertaking very time-intensive individualized counseling and visitation. While the congregation as a whole was "progressive" and the majority of its members did not worry about such things as the gender of their pastors, some members preferred a man for a pastor, proudly calling themselves "old-fashioned," at least in this respect. In any case, all tried to accept each others' preferences. June and John worked together so well that even the "old-fashioned" members eventually wound up appreciating the presence of both pastors at births, weddings, funerals, family crises, and so forth. After trying to keep up with this desire of the congregation, John and June found themselves exhausted from too much work together. They realized that they could be more effective and could cover more ground if they split up their responsibilities. Their communication was excellent. They could disagree with one another without rancor and really enjoyed being with each other.

After two years of ministry together June began to feel uneasy about her relationship with John. She noticed that she spent far more time with John than with Jerry or their children. She confided in John about her worries as much as she did with her husband because John was a good listener. She recognized that she and John had a kind of "intimate" relationship, which while not sexually active, was profoundly close. She searched her feelings and realized that she had a great deal of "love" for John, and this worried her a great deal. Was this strong feeling for John in conflict with her marriage vows to Jerry? What about John's wife, Rita? They were great friends, often kidding one another about how John really had two wives! But was Rita jealous of the time June shared with John? Cominformstry involved a bond that seemed precariously close to that of marriage, or at least a marriage without vows.

John had similar concerns. He was a very "huggy" kind of extrovert. Lately, however, he had not felt comfortable with hugging his colleague June because of the way that June held on to him. Well, he held on to her a little bit longer than they had before, too, if truth be told. . . . He wondered about his powerful feelings of closeness to June, because he really loved Rita, and Jerry was his closest friend. Was their closeness a kind of betrayal of their wedding vows? How do we "cling unto" our spouses while working closely with someone of the opposite sex?

John and June talked with their spouses about their concerns. They were honest about their feelings for each other. To their great surprise they found out that Rita and Jerry had recently spoken about their own worries in this regard. They had noticed that John and June seemed like a "married couple," and they felt "left out" from the pastors' jokes. Jerry was jealous of the time that John had with June, and Rita was jealous of June's "great looks" (something she had never confided to John in all the years that the four had known one another), and she also noticed the long hugs shared between them.

All four decided to have a joint dinner and talk things out.

This case raises various issues that can be easily framed as a part of the Journey moralscape. The moralscape is a way of describing what goes on in an ethical dilemma, but it is most effective as a *practical tool for interrogating and analyzing a situation.* When one uses the moralscape as a tool of interrogation and analysis, a few procedural suggestions are in order:

Always ask questions, get more information. The more data you can compile about the situation, the better you will be able to understand what cultural logics, values, norms, and loyalties actually underlie the apparent conflict in the situation.

Use the categories of the moralscape as a way of systematically analyzing the situation. For example, what are the moral metaphysics of John and June? That is to say, what qualities of character, virtue, and moral agency can we discern about them from the case story as it is? What do you think they would identify as the moral *telos* of their actions as ministers? What questions would you want to ask of them? How do you suppose that they would answer your questions? Then, one could move on to the next category—a critical theory of society and culture. What are the cultural logics operative in the behaviors and conversations of John and June, Jerry and Rita? Can we tell anything about their attitudes toward "valorizing cultural difference?" Are there indications of their awareness of the *habitus* of appropriate male-female interaction? What types of capital do each of the four main agents in this ethical dilemma display? Do they demonstrate an "explicit awareness of the political and economic system that influences our ideas of the good?" Is there any sort of systematic theological articulation present in their dilemma? What questions would you ask them in order to get at their views of God, humanity, the problem of sin, and so forth?

Be imaginative. Sometimes the most obvious "answers" to a moralscape's interrogation are not true to the intention of the moral actors. Thus, one must consider a variety of factors that might explain why, for example, none of these persons suggested that they pray about the situation. No one specifically mentioned God, either. Is that strange for a group of Christian ministers, or is it so presupposed that it never arose explicitly? Or is the absence of language about prayer indicative of the kind of spirituality practiced by John, June, Rita, and Jerry?

Remember that you are interrogating someone else's moralscape from the vantage point of your own moralscape. Remain self-conscious. Note the little details that are left out and the way in which details are presented.

Deconstruct and reconstruct the scenario. Talk through alternative ways of posing the problem. Do not be afraid to ask "What if" questions because such speculation can help us interpret and isolate the moment(s) in which certain moral choices suddenly became ethical demands requiring action. For example, if John did not hug June so much, would there have been any reason for either person to wonder about the direction of their professional association? *Specify the categories of moralscape analysis to fit the particular case.* For example, certain assumptions of formality and professionalism, of "professional ethics," are directly related to some of the problems presented in this case study. It is widely discouraged in the contemporary mixed-gender workplace for persons to greet one another with hugs, kisses, or other signs of affection that could be construed as overtly sexual. One would need to contrast this particular aspect of cultural logics with the common ethos of many churchfolk, particularly those of a charismatic bent like John and June, which encourages "holy hugs" as a sign between the "brothers and sisters in Christ." By specifying the manner in which these two commonly understood moral practices have collided in the situation of John and June, we uncover some of the "dirtiness" residing at the heart of such matters. Remember, if things were clear-cut, then none of the parties involved in this case would ever have felt so uneasy. Further, this case has to do with *sexuality*—one of the most volatile ethical topics, for Christians in particular. The matter of sexuality and sexual ethics is significant enough to warrant a separate discussion. How can we speak of the holiness of our bodies and our feelings when so much of Christian history has derided all forms of sexuality as bestial, "fleshly," carnal, and sinful?

SEXUAL ETHICS IN A CONFLICTED SOCIETY

Womanist ethicist Emilie Townes has noted that the contemporary ethos of the United States is in a state of dangerous moral schizophrenia. It is a conflicted, self-contradictory ethos that simultaneously proclaims sexual repression and sexual promiscuity.[1] Ours is a nation that takes pride in its spiritual holiness, presenting itself to the world as a "Christian country," and pride in its political righteousness as a home of "freedom and democracy." At the same time we are a nation overwhelmed by an objectifying "gaze" in regard to public displays of sexuality. Encouraging the sexualization of bodies (particularly female bodies), the hedonist impulses of consumerism are rigorously enforced by an advertisement-driven media, in which the everyday coinage sells objectified "sex" as a way of expanding market share. We all know that the worth of a car, a razor, or a drink cannot be accurately measured by the promise of sexual availability and attractiveness implied in commercials! Yet market forces have debased sexuality on a massive and public scale.

Those who follow Jesus in such a society necessarily find ourselves resisting the dehumanizing postures and pictures and the messages of unlimited sexual availability promoted throughout our culture. This brings us to the other side of the unhappy dialectic—sexual repression. While on the one hand, comedians make crude sexual jokes, on the other hand, their jibes also broadcast and legitimate the neo-Puritanical sexual repression sweeping our nation since the mid 1980s. President Bill Clinton was castigated (and even impeached) for issues surrounding sexual impropriety, and at the same time he was tacitly applauded for his sexual peccadilloes, as expressed in the grudging admiration of comedians and talk-show hosts. Such "schizophrenic" behavior suggests a society deeply conflicted about its views of the body, sexuality, and appropriate boundaries.

In my Journey model of ethics, I try to resacralize the body and sexuality in a way that does not repress sexual expressiveness. As a follower of Jesus whose primary authority in these matters is the Bible, it is clear to me that God created our bodies as part of the holy work of creation (Gen. 1 and 2). Being "created in the image of God" means more than being "rational" (as the Enlightenment legacy insists). Woven into the very fibers of our human being is an urge to connect, relate, and love one another. We express this fundamental aspect of ourselves through language, through actions, and, perhaps most intimately, through touch. Just as God "touched" the earth, shaped it, and "breathed into it the breath of life" (*nephesh* in Hebrew), so we touch and breathe love into one another's lives. Our bodies, in all of their various shapes, skin colors, eye proportions, nose shapes, lip sizes, and other proportions and aspects, are the "tents" for our spirits—that same "holy stuff" breathed into Adam and Eve in the very origin of our creation as human beings. We use this tent to reveal our deepest purposes, values, loyalties, and feelings. Further, our capacity to experience emotion is as much a part of the *imago dei* as is our faculty of reasoning and our fundamental need to connect, relate, and love.

All three of these aspects—reason, emotion, and the need for connection, relation, love—are *embodied*. We express them *in* our bodies, *with* our bodies. We do not pronounce our feelings, our ideas, and our needs from some disembodied "no place." We are *somewhere*. That *somewhere* is our body. Therefore, any strong feelings of connection and relation with anyone else are an aspect of that fundamental urge to connect and relate. Such an urge ought not to be reduced to the instinctual drives of reproduction. Theologically, it is part of that continuum of love aspects mentioned in chapter 4—from the most overtly sexual *epithymia* (sexual, reproductive love) to the most overtly mystical *agape*.

We notice one another's bodies just as much as we hear words, see colors, and feel the air rushing across our skin. It is not sinful to notice each other's bodies as we communicate. So where can sinfulness enter the picture? Where's the dirt?

The dirt (in this case, exploitation) is in our caving into an objectified "gaze" upon one another. The gaze comes from an ethos that historically "evaluated" the bodies, teeth, muscles, and work and reproductive abilities of African bodies as they stood on display in auction blocks. For some four hundred years this kind of gaze was directed at black bodies. For even a longer stretch of time—going back further than we can easily locate, the bodies of women have been paraded before the appraising eyes of men. Such "appraisal" degraded women's dignity, turning creatures of God's grace and image into mere vehicles for physical pleasure and/or reproduction.

As a minister of the gospel of Jesus Christ, I believe that we ought to teach our children that sexuality is a good and natural part of their God-given humanity. It is such a precious and special gift that I believe it is totally appropriate for us to encourage our young folks to abstain from fully expressing themselves sexually until they are in a committed relationship. I know that such counsel could be subverted by the wiles of a lying man or woman, but it is a fair counsel. It recognizes that sexuality is a gift best left unopened until one is in a committed relationship, while recognizing that we live in a time in which the definition of a "committed relationship" is being radically questioned, as in nontraditional covenant services and in same-sex unions. We cannot overlook such unions, nor can we simply condemn them. Such an ethics is too easy, undisciplined, and unwilling to struggle with the fray of ever-changing life. On the middle-way journey we are willing to engage in open debate about the meaning of a committed relationship for Christians. Some of us will define a committed relationship in the traditional terms of heterosexual unions between one woman and one man. Others will really throw that definition wide open.

Theologically, and ethically, the most important thing to note is that our sexuality is as much a gift of God as any other aspect of our humanity, and therefore it is not something that should be repressed, suppressed, or ignored. As such, it must be handled with great care, sensitivity, and open communication. No one should ever be "approached" sexually; sexual expression is an exercise in profound, mutual, relational communication. To experience a "come-on" is to be objectified, made into the object of someone else's fantasies, hopes, and desires. Finally, as Marie Fortune clearly states, professional relations ought never to be sexualized, because they involve an inherent power differential that can so easily lead to an exploitative dynamic.[2]

What a middle-way Christian ethic like the Journey moralscape model suggests is that we need to teach young people and see ourselves as unavoidably sexual, even as we are spiritual, emotional, and reasonable. This self image has an extremely important function in everyday communication between persons—whatever their sexual orientation or gender identification. If being sexual is a part of the way that I am "in the world," then sexuality is as valuable an aspect of my holiness as any other aspect of my humanity. It is as sacred as prayer, as expressive as feelings, and as ennobling as reason. Sexuality, when viewed through such a lens, is inevitably a part of our everyday interactions.

If being sexual is part of the way that human bodies interact, what about John and June? Do we simply tell them to "go with the flow"? Or do we tell them to "be careful"? There is no quick and easy answer to John and June's case. They have followed the dictates of their uneasy consciences and have talked separately and together with their spouses. Their honesty suggests a real desire that virtue be in the foreground of their relationship, thus curbing the possibility of a secretive "love affair." No secret can be hidden for very long, anyway. Once all of the feelings are "out on the table," God willing, all parties can continue to hold one another up in prayer. Prayer, fellowship, and open communication is what I would urge, along with gratitude that both John and June clearly value their married relationships as most important.

From the viewpoint of professional ethics, John probably needs to re-examine his "huggy" character, both in light of the effect that his hugs apparently have had on June and in light of the possibility that his hugs might cause further problems for other women (and men) in their congregation.

The Pauline missionary injunction "Be all things to all persons" ought to be reconstrued and expanded in our era to include the new "facts" of our social life. As men and women work together, sometimes as closely as John and June, certain kinds of physical touch may need to be re-evaluated in light of their potential for being misunderstood as sexual advances. In a professional arena as personal and close as pastoral ministry, professionals must not place themselves and others into sexualized positions. Will this change the informality of many workplaces? Undoubtedly it will, in that boundaries will become very clear. However, we can be certain that by desexualizing our workplaces, we will also be reinserting the presence of a balance between love, power, and justice. The ways in which our sexuality, spirituality, and emotions interact make us vulnerable to potentially exploitative relations rather than relations of admirable justice and holiness. In order for genuine justice to occur in the workplace, or in this case, in a church community, we can restrain sexualized touching without devaluing the concrete good that is touch. A Journey model ought to explore ways in which touch can be experienced as healing and supportive without the threat of sexual exploitation. Statistically, one of every four women in ministry has experienced unwanted sexual advances, rape, incest, or some other form of sexual abuse. With such a massive social problem, ministers like John and June have a unique opportunity to model professional friendship (including appropriate touching) for their congregation. Invariably this will lead to some radical rethinking and new practices of demonstrating support, affection, and care.

FOR FURTHER REFLECTION

1. In your opinion, how do sexuality and gender roles relate in other settings? In school, work, family, and elsewhere? Which of these also involve questions of power?

2. How does sexuality figure in the political and economic systems discussed in chapter 4? Are some images and expectations of what it means to be a man or woman encouraged, tolerated, or disapproved by commercial or political communications? Examples?

CHAPTER 6

Real Dirt: Getting Our Hands Dirty with Life

Dirty hands cannot be holy hands unless they are involved in generating concrete, pragmatic answers to that stirring question, "So what?" It is a demand to "be real," as the black folks who raised me would probably ask of me. What difference can we make in the world when we know that despite our most sincere intentions, heartfelt hopes and prayers, we cannot commit ourselves to any creative good without getting dirty hands? Because God created us from the dust and earth and because we are spiritually shaped Earth creatures, the daring heart of any important ethical dilemma demands that we get our hands dirtied with life's ambiguities.

Does admitting that ethics and decision making are one of life's most murky realities lead us to apathy? Some people are afraid to act because their choices might have ambiguous or negative or unforeseen consequences. They might even fall into the moral pitfall of despair and cynicism. Yet, aren't Christians supposed to be the ones who bring holiness, purity, and light to a so-called dark world?

The aim of this book is to dare us to choose and to act, even if doing so means that our apathetic and uninvolved hands will become dirty as they participate in making holy decisions based on our faith in Jesus. To be a follower of Jesus inevitably entails getting dirty in the real social, political, emotional, and psychological dramas that God places us in as friends, family, coworkers, employers, leaders, and followers. God has not promised us a dirt-free existence. Rather, God has promised to accompany our stumbling ambiguous choices and bend them toward a righteous end. In a word, our engaged, dirty-hands choices are part of the very process of sanctification and transformation that God challenges us to embody.

THE JOURNEY OF HOLINESS

We are not allowed the luxury of disengagement from life's ambiguous choices. The journey of holiness is an arduous path leading us toward the gospel ideal of "abundant life" so beautifully described in the Gospel of John 10:10, "The thief comes only to steal and kill and destroy. I came that they might have life, and have it abundantly." This ideal of abundance is not only the holy end that the journey of holiness leads us toward, but also it is the complex and sometimes confusing regulating norm or means by which we move toward a sanctified life. All of our choices, no matter how simple or complex, are conformed to God's presence. As such, every choice poses the hard question, "In what way can this choice and situation become an example of God's abundant life?"

We are not alone on our journey. The paths we wander are not filled with endless questions that appear to confirm the truth of absolute ethical relativism. Stumbling along, we meet each other across the chasm of multicultural differences and social practices that seems so wide that we may be incapable of reaching a genuine agreement. What is our role as followers of Jesus on this journey of holiness? We are called into a middle way, a way of diligently seeking God's will in every particular situation (as Bonhoeffer suggested). Yet our attention to the particularities of the situation does not change our normative question, "In what way can my choice become an example of God's abundant life?"

To be guided by a normative question is to be compelled both in conscience and body to be active agents who take irrevocable responsibility for our active choices. God's agency energizes and "quickens" (to use an archaic English term) our human moral agency. God's power is not devalued, nor is God's love constrained if we take upon ourselves the responsibility of acting with hands that have been dirtied in the hustle and bustle of everyday life.

JOURNEYING TOWARD PERFECTION. Our unique and irrevocable responsibility is a high calling also to choose actively for the entire creation, and not just for our own particular human needs. In fact, each of us is God's created worker, stepping forward into the dirty realm of concrete choices. With prayer, meditation, and sometimes even fasting, we still stand responsibly aware that we will inevitably become dirty as we engage in, sift through, gather evidence, and eventually come down on one side or the other. We perceive God's agency in this journey of holiness only through the committed and steadfast faith that urges us to move forward, to keep on going. This responsibility cannot be understood in long-winded philosophical abstractions meaningful only to those elite intellectuals initiated into the mysteries of so-called higher, critical thinking. Rather, our dirty hands deal in nitty-gritty, everyday choices. Everyday questions have moral significance. Should I work all day for my family, or take the day off? What do *I* need for myself? Would the family feel hurt if they found out that I had gone off to the beach by myself?

Our faith is a lifelong journey toward holiness. But what do we mean by *holiness?* Are we speaking about being "clean" or "spotless" in the presence of the pure God? In some ways, yes, but an emphasis on ideas of holiness as cleanliness has easily degenerated historically into grand social programs that uplifted one ethnicity (for example, as Nazis held up the "Aryan ideal") as superior to and dominant over all other ethnicities. When cleanliness becomes the primary aim of holiness, dangerous ideals of dominance, power-over, and expanding empires seem to follow.[1]

On the other hand, if holiness implies that lifelong journey of sanctification that John Wesley called "perfection," we have different strengths and problems to deal with. Clearly Wesley's call to aim for perfection is not a demand that we attain a state of sinlessness, inerrancy, and moral superiority (although some may have believed that of Wesley). Rather, Wesley's description of perfection emphasizes the following points:

- The mature or "grown Christian" achieves perfection in the sense of being "freed from evil thoughts and evil tempers."
- Christian perfection is positively stated in "Christ liveth in me" and negatively clarified in the Pauline verse, "I am crucified with Christ; nevertheless I live; yet not I, but Christ liveth in me." Wesley saw these words as manifestly describing "a deliverance from inward as well as from outward sin."
- Thus a mature Christian is purified by Christ living within to live freed from pride, "for Christ was lowly in heart." This purification

ends "desire and self-will" because "Christ desired only to do the will of his Father." Finally, the one moving in God's purified "perfection" emulates Christ's meekness and gentleness by being "pure from anger."[2]

- Finally, Wesley implies that perfection is a synonym for the life-long process of *sanctification* (being made holy by God's grace), but he is never clear about either the existence of "degrees of perfection" or whether its highest "degree" would be at the moment of one's death.[3]

PERFECTION FOR "THE CHALLENGED." We move along our journey of holiness in halting, sometimes crippled ways. As one who is intermittently "disabled" or "physically challenged," I can testify to the frustrating depths of the experience of not being "able" to do with my body what my mind has chosen or even "commanded" my body to do. As one whose physical condition has led to bouts of acute clinical depression and bi-polarity, I can also testify to the agony of wanting to do and choose the right thing, but not possessing the mental powers whereby I can actually do that which I know to be right and good. It is aggravating, physically and mentally, to possess the desire to do something only to find that hobbled legs, painful joints, or an enervated mind interfere with the execution of the act.

In God's grace it is possible for those like myself still to see themselves as active choosers, created by God to make a difference in the world. My halting physical steps and occasional mental anguish are but material expressions of what it seems all human beings are compelled to face when we take the journey of holiness seriously. We do not pass through this "veil of tears" without various wounds of body, mind, soul, and spirit.

DIRT AND OTHERS

As God calls us forward into the "adventure"[4] that is the journey of holiness, we find our lives getting ever more deeply engaged in the dirty stuff that is life. Moving onward, we are pressed to consider more than our individual status and place before our maker. Somehow the journey moves us outward, beyond the safety of familiar faces, places, and feelings. Our journey draws us outward to gaze into the faces of others, to recognize their "otherness" as a demand for our attention and care. As Emmanuel Levinas has pointed out, it is in the encounter with the "face of the Other" that we are called to "responsibility."[5] For Levinas all philosophy (a term that encompasses theology and life itself) starts with the basic is-ness of the face-to-face encounter. Its irreducibility, its facticity calls us outside of our introverted cycles of self-affirmation, outward toward the heights where we can recognize the "self" in the facing of "the Other" (in French, *l'Autrui*).

One cannot make hasty judgments about the strangeness, or beauty, or even repulsion one feels about any Other,—homosexuals, dark-skinned peoples, outspoken women, assertive children—if one has not had a face-to-face encounter with a living, breathing human being labeled as Other. Somehow, all of our facile biblical quotes, prejudgments based on second- and third-hand stories, and natural prejudices shift under the very humanity of the gaze shared between oneself and the Other. For Levinas, the thing we call our "self" can never be the same once we have truly faced the face of an Other and have recognized our fundamental responsibility to that person as a living being. For example, our easily held prejudices about all of the "them" out there tend to dissolve in the concrete, dirty, face-to-face encounter with another human being. The journey toward holiness not only morally perfects us, but also it widens our cosmos of compassion. In fact, once the cosmos of one's moral and spiritual compassion has been opened up, it is hard to look at a flower, tree, sky, or mountain without standing in awe of the majestic holiness of ordinary creation—human or otherwise. Still, some are afraid to open themselves to this adventurous journey. For such as these, we gently apply our critical theories in hopes that hearts and attitudes will open rather than close.

EARTH AS OTHER

The Earth is an Other that, until recently, traditional Christian ethics has failed to honor. On the Journey of holiness we are challenged to face her in a variety of ancient namings—*terra firma*, or Gaia, or Mother. The Earth is a living, dynamic, complex, and yet fragile interlocking biological organism, according to biologists Lynn Margulis and James

Lovelock.[6] Our bodies emerge from this living, dynamic, complex, and fragile biochemical interaction as from a living being, our Mother, Gaia. Our bodies are *of* the Earth, they are comprised of the same elements and biochemical interactions that are found in Gaia. So, in a very profound sense, we *are* Earth because she courses through us as life itself.

Holiness can be embraced if we recognize the fact of our *Earth-ness*. Too much traditional theology and ethics have emphasized the human role as "stewards," as the dominating creatures of *terra firma*, standing as some kind of transcendent beings "above" and "apart" from the dirt of the Earth. The Bible (Gen. 1:26-28; 2:7), in contrast, reminds us that our theological origins are found in our being created "in the image of God," lovingly crafted by God's "hands" from the "dust of the earth." We are Earth, in all of our glorious, conflictual differences. Paul recast the same thought in the New Testament by noting that human beings are "treasures in earthen vessels" (2 Cor. 4:7). We are God's treasures in "clay jars." Earlier descriptions of this wondrous "two-ness," this spiritual and physical nature, envision human beings as created with both biochemical, natural, and historical elements and a transcendent, God-implanted essence.[7] The wisdom of Lovelock's and Margulis's "Gaia hypothesis" lies in its reclamation of the immanent and transcendent divine elements into an Earth-based holiness. Likewise, the growing corpus of ecological writings by esteemed feminist Christians like Sallie McFague and Rosemary Radford Ruether boldly proclaim notions of holiness that connect Earth with human beings and all of creation itself.[8]

Human beings are immanent and transcendent creatures. The results of our behavior—in evil pollution, befouled air, and poisoned waters—affect nature immanently and transcendentally. We are neither miniature gods trapped in base and crude physicality, nor dualized beings whose two distinct aspects act in perpetual conflict with each other. Rather, we are God's creation, fashioned with the same holy care with which God fashioned Gaia. Further, we can make choices that increase our holiness by re-establishing a meaningful and respectful relationship with the body of Gaia, of which we are a part. Affirming our connection to Earth, to Gaia, reveals a willingness to be both spiritual and physical beings. Holy life begins by risking the dirty-hands choices of this immediate life, and this does not really subvert or contradict the holiness of our spirits living on eternally, even after our flesh bodies die. Life, death, and rebirth are inescapable aspects of the cyclical or circular trajectory of life, so a journey of holiness revalues the holiness of bodies, even as they move and breathe on Earth.

BODY AS OTHER. We are each entrusted with the body is that Other as we travel life's paths. Its ties to the micro-organisms produced by Gaia make life's journey quite difficult upon occasion because we suffer from the effects of viruses, bacteria, and the eventual toxicity of human-developed antigens. That is the point. We suffer in our bodies—whether physically, emotionally, in our soul (personality), or spiritually. As Gaia experiences suffering on the macro-level, from drought, blight, famine, and plague, so our bodies analogously suffer on the micro-level. Yet the puzzle remains. Why has God entrusted God's "image" inside these fragile bodies?

On the journey of holiness we may find that God's gracious answer to this last question is simply to affirm the body as our sacred house. The holiness of our physical lives is an immeasurably wonderful gift from God. When we have traveled on the journey of holiness long enough, we come to realize the preciousness of the most simple things. We rejoice in the freshness of the air because we perceive it through our senses, as when after a strong rain our noses smell it, our skin feels it, and our eyes see it. We give thanks after coming through snowstorms, tornadoes, hurricanes, fires, earthquakes, and other natural disasters because our bodies provide the rest of our being with the information to let us know that the danger has passed over. God apparently wants us to experience the journey of holiness in a body, and so our body-houses are sacred. Our body-houses are holy because they both *contain* and *are* us.

ENVIRONMENTAL ABUSE. Environmental abuse is the exploitative intervention of human technology and its wastes into nature's cycles of life. A middle-way Journey ethic cannot make wide-eyed condemnations of technology as unqualified evil, since we recognize that one of the distinctive gifts of being created in the image of the Creator is the same creativity that created technology. *Homo sapiens* is also *homo technologicus* (technological human). Thus, technological development—from the most primitive transformation of bones into hammers (and hunting weapons) to construction of the most intricate spacecraft—is an integral part of what it means to be human. Technology stands alongside art, music, dance, writing, engineering, and architecture as an example of human creativity. So one cannot make a facile blanket condemnation of technology. Rather, on the journey toward holiness we prayerfully insist that technological developments and innovations be able to stand under the critical scrutiny of life-affirming ethical standards. When we look at the ethical conflicts arising from the accomplishments of genetic engineering, for example, a Journey ethic reminds geneticists that every "advance" and "gain" in our knowledge of the intricacies of the genetic helix of life expresses the God-given drive toward creative inquisitiveness and constructive intelligence. At the same time, a Journey ethic reminds us all of that along this path of creative inquisitiveness lay ambiguities and dangers that may become destructive and inimical to God's creation. Human creativity participates in the ambiguity of dirty hands.

Scripturally we might add that the Genesis 2 "blessing" of human beings to have "dominion" over the earth represents this strange admixture of human creative traits. This norm of *dominion,* which contemporary Bible scholars have softened to mean *stewardship,* does not preclude the sin of arrogance, as human beings take the lead over the rest of creation. Not only do we name objects, plants, animals, and other things, but we seem driven to do so! A Journey ethic reminds those who attempt to be followers of Jesus that whether we call it *dominion* or *stewardship,* the Bible speaks of a peculiar trait within human beings, an admixture of curiosity with creativity and a moral compass that can be properly used or perverted.

As part of our curious "dominion" capacity, we tamper and pry into the very processes of life itself, with both good and evil intentions. To decry genetic engineering or other technological interventions as messing with business that belongs only to God is to miss the nuance of the dominion/stewardship insight into human character. Such unthinking criticism is as laughable as saying, "If we had been intended to fly, God would have given us wings!"—quite a popular statement before the twentieth century. Rather, on the journey, we compel scientific advances to answer several fundamental queries into the basic assumptions and probable outcomes of our society's ongoing commitment to genetic engineering (or any such technology):

What is the aim of such a technological breakthrough or advance?
This simple query is often overlooked when we are bound up in the sensationalism of the media moment. Consider, for example, the sheep
"Dolly," the first complete higher mammal to result from the cloning
procedure. When Dolly's birth was announced in 1997, questions about
the purpose of cloning technology seemed to dim in light of our amaze-
ment at the story itself. Instead, we could and should be asking the genetic engineering community if their aim is to improve the human food
supply of sheep or to develop stronger sheep (as carefully controlled
breeding has done for many generations)? Are we nudging nature's reproductive processes because we are self-aware, curious creatures of nature, or are we ultimately trying to gain a frightening capacity to control
all forms of reproduction? Conspiracy theorists and imaginative sci-
ence-fiction writers may envision future corporations developing virtually "perfect" human beings as a way of maintaining a highly engineered
elite population's utter control over those who have not been engineered.[9] Would we not call such an application of genetic engineering
"evil" and work against it? Speculation is already heating up about the
implications of cloning entire human bodies for the sole purpose of
"harvesting" their organs for the desperately sick. Would our aim in such
a practice be to aid medical science "by every means available," or
would we force ourselves to ask about whether these "harvest clones"
were human? If we agreed that they were human, then what "inalien-
able rights" (as the phrase goes in the Declaration of Independence)
would they have? Further interrogation would peel away possible class
interests. How wealthy would one need to be to afford a "cloned part"?
Would the federal or state governments take decisive steps in making
cloned organs a universal health right, or would the lobbyists of the most
privileged preclude such discussions from ever reaching a vote? By
asking about the aim of technological projects on a case-by-case basis,
especially projects as potentially significant as genetic cloning, we preserve our ability to carefully approve and disapprove certain uses and
abuses.

Why is this technological application being pursued? Is it the only
way, or even the best way, of approaching the problem? Christian ethicists cannot stand on the sidelines of scientific and technological development, wringing our hands and spouting Scriptures indiscriminately.

A Journey model of Christian ethics gives itself permission to interrogate technological interventions and applications aggressively, using the tools of Scripture, reason, experience, and tradition. *Who will benefit from this technological breakthrough?* This is the key question that a Journey model can pose. It can be easily observed that the *habitus* of most of the developed world includes reliance on technological discovery, application, and renovation. The computer stands as the foremost example of how innovation and variation create more demand. One purchases a state-of-the-art personal computer in September, and by January of the next year, the next generation of state-of-the-art computing has already made one's relatively new computer outdated! Trying to avoid the shame of owning a "dinosaur," we try to purchase an expandable hardware format that we can keep "updated" with so-called upgrades. Since the ethos of the computer user's *habitus* encourages continuous advancement, current practices of computer ownership require owners to run continually down to the nearest computer supermarket to get the newest and latest technological innovations. While a description of this frenetic practice is almost comical, prohibitive pricing makes this feature of "modern" life a most subtle form of torture.

Followers of Jesus who are familiar with the saying of Jesus "You cannot serve God and wealth" (Matt. 6:24) may recognize the inherent dissonance between the frenetic *habitus*/ethos of technological innovation and the ethos of Jesus. Jesus' *habitus* and ethos are expressed magnificently in the Sermon on the Mount: "Do not worry about tomorrow, for tomorrow has enough worries of its own" (Matt. 6:34). Once we recognize the dissonance between these two conflicting forms of practice and value, something ought to move us to criticize the corporate practice of manufacturing newer and newer products, which in turn feeds consumer appetites for owning the latest gadget. Bolstered with our critical suspicions, followers of Jesus ought to initiate conversations that question the need for faster and faster microchips, especially in light of their prohibitive prices. This is a question of distributive justice.

Unfortunately, the ethical choice has already been concretized into practice; the computer industry has decided that producing more capacious, faster, and smaller products for those who can afford them is more important than developing low-priced and universally available technologies for all classes of people. Therefore the high-tech era is dominated by the wealthy and highly educated. Access to the Internet, fax machines, and powerful laptop computers remains an assumed possession of the middle to upper classes, while the masses struggle to gain basic equipment from among the "hand-me-downs" of the affluent. In the United States of America many African American, Latino/Latina, and poor Asian communities are still underrepresented on the growing "information highway." Like so many other thoroughfares of life, this superhighway of turbocharged microchips seems to have bypassed poor communities. Has the information superhighway already established "tolls and fees" far too high for the majority to afford? Ought not Christian ethicists to be the ones to ask these questions, providing a voice for those who are marginalized far from the boardrooms?

Is a high level of technological intervention effectively abusing the larger ecology of life? Our capacity to intervene radically in the natural ecology of foodstuffs can be most easily represented by the genetically enhanced tomato. Developed to have a greater resistance to rotting, these tomatoes hardly ever rot before being harvested, or even after being picked, packaged, and placed on market counters. In the natural cycle, as I learned through years of growing tomatoes with my father, soil is replenished by rotting vegetation. Rotting tomatoes underneath the vines have a critically important function in ensuring the soil's fertility. This cycle has been disrupted in "enhanced" tomato fields, lowering the quality of the soil. Rotten tomatoes, the unsalable portion of the crop, serve to feed the dirt that produced them, but engineered tomatoes increase the picked crop's profitability, staying fresher and tastier on store shelves for a longer period of time. From a strictly economic point of view, genetically engineered tomatoes are marvelous, but from an ecological viewpoint, they may not be the ultimate miracle plant. We may need to revalue the role of rotting tomatoes in maintaining tomato production, with some kind of balance between natural and engineered tomatoes.

Recognizing this need may provoke us into organized economic resistance, boycotting altered tomatoes. We can also look ahead to the long-term consequences. To rephrase the ancient prophets, quick gains that do not count the cost of possible outcomes can turn into permanent losses. If soil is overused, it will require other kinds of fertilization to replenish its productive capacity. As farmers strive to maintain the high profitability of engineered produce, the soil may become toxic from overfertilization by chemicals other than those naturally produced in rotting tomatoes. If the soil becomes toxic, it will bear nothing, and a rapid demise in economic profitability will aid neither corporations nor consumers. Such an outcome would surely be contrary to long-term profitability! Thus, if we look ahead to possible outcomes, our argument can engage an economic issue in economic terms for the sake of a healthier ecology.

ENVIRONMENTAL RACISM. Environmental abuse accentuates abusive patterns of racism already embedded in the social fabric. Three out of every five black and Latino/Latina Americans live in communities with uncontrolled toxic waste sites.[10] Of fifty metropolitan areas with the highest number of African Americans, some 75.3 percent have "new" uncontrolled toxic waste sites. In ten of these metropolitan areas, over 90 percent of the African American population lies near uncontrolled waste sites. Memphis, Tennessee, is the most glaring example, with an "estimated 99.8 percent of its African American population residing in areas of uncontrolled sites."[11]

Comparable patterns of environmental racism exist for Hispanic Americans, so that in "at least six metropolitan areas," "more than 100,000 Hispanics" are "living in communities with uncontrolled toxic waste sites."[12] Some 75 percent of the residents in rural areas of the Southwest, mainly Hispanics, are drinking pesticide-contaminated water. Native Americans suffer from the effects of "2 million tons of uranium tailings" dumped on their reservations," and as a result, Navajo teenagers have seventeen times the national average of organ cancers."[13]

For poor people and people of color, environmental abuse has concrete health consequences. Cynthia Hamilton notes that in 1986, black and Latina women organized to stop the LANCER (Los Angeles City Energy Recovery Project), a thirteen-acre incinerator that would "burn 2,000 tons a day of municipal waste." The Los Angeles City Council had already determined that LANCER should be built in the predominantly African American and Hispanic south central area of the city. The proposed LANCER stacks would have pumped dioxins and mercury, among other toxins, into the air.[14]

Most of the women (and men) had only high school education or less, were unemployed, and had little of the economic resources usually available to middle and upper-class organizers. Yet these residents of South Central Los Angeles realized that "somebody's going to be affected,"[15] even though they were bombarded by testimony from scientific authorities, which was meant to allay their fears. Eventually the city council, tired of being "patient," became dismissive of the residents' honest questions. Against the cumulative evidence compiled by the council's "experts," the anti-LANCER organization was actually galvanized by the insulting attitudes of the city's authorities. For example, when one "expert witness" noted that the "health risks associated with dioxin exposure were less than those associated with eating peanut butter," the crowd rose up in angry furor. Inciting the wrath of an organized resistance group, other "experts" spoke of congenital deformities and cancers as "acceptable risks." This kind of information convinced the mothers to make even more impassioned pleas concerning their families' health issues—"a child's asthma, or a parent's influenza, or the high rate of cancer, heart disease, and pneumonia" already prevalent "in this poverty-stricken community."[16] In the end, the courage and passionate, organized pleas of the anti-LANCER group finally aroused enough anger in the middle- to upper-class women's groups and other civic associations that the proposal was defeated. Unfortunately, such victories are still the exception to the norm rather than common practice.

Being aware of environmental racism also involves learning about the harshness of lead poisoning. In 1988, for example, the federal Agency for Toxic Substances and Disease Registry noted that "for families earning less that $6,000 annually, an estimated 68 percent of African American children had lead poisoning, compared with 36 percent for white children."[17] Explanations for lead poisoning, which increases the risk of learning disabilities and mental retardation, appear at the intersection of classism and racism, but the race variable is significant enough to be noticeable. On our journey, we cannot ignore the admixture of classism, racism, and simple avarice that affect the plight of the poor. Rather, a Journey model attempts to highlight the interests of the poor, an especially important socioeconomic and cultural group that requires the attention of the followers of Jesus. That more than one-third of the white

American population suffers from the blight of lead poisoning ought to outrage us to collective action, not to mention the two-thirds of impoverished black, brown, and red children who likewise suffer.

One might wonder to what end I am devoting so much space to citing figures. Do the figures "prove" the point by themselves? My point is to make an argument that will encourage us to collectively rise up together, bridging forces across ethnic and racial[18] boundaries. Do I intend to "make whites feel guilty," as one particularly sensitive student tearfully expressed? No. Rather, this information is meant to provide a concrete example of the ways in which *empirical* and *experiential data* must be developed and deployed in persuasive moral argumentation. We need more information about the pragmatic concerns of everyday urban and rural people (as well as their suburban counterparts) because the health, livelihoods, and homes of all of us are threatened by the profligate abuse of our natural environments. There is no vacation spot or national park that is not also befouled by polluted air and toxic water.[19]

Environmental issues are not the abstract, intellectual "playthings" of college elitists; they involve the everyday life and death situations faced by all of us. Our empirical data cannot actually persuade a reader of anything unless there is a social-justice imperative that walks with us through the morass of numbers. Ultimately the statistics say that we are all being affected in negative ways by the unrestrained rape of Gaia. The usage of "rape" rhetoric is intentional, for we are forcibly abusing this celestial body, this planet that provides us with life and energy, this home that we have been entrusted to preserve, steward, and manage. It is imperative for all of us to receive and act on the truth that Gaia and humanity are one, that our common preservation should be considered primary, and that our survival is the most important order of global business.

TOUCHING GAIA: RELIGIONS OF THE WORLD. The Earth, Gaia, is being raped and abused. Despite this stunning assertion, one might ask (especially if one is among those human beings most marginalized by the powerful), "So what?" The very question shuts down our imaginative capacities. Besides, we rationalize to ourselves, we have "more immediately important things to do." We might go so far as to ask,

"What does summoning conflicted groups of the poor and rich, the light and dark, female and male together to stop these abuses require of me?" But eventually we tend to turn all moral reasoning back to our individual desires and needs. Where do we find the resources to reach out across our self-centered fears and face the global ecological crises together—as a human family? Beyond that vital first step, how can we develop the wherewithal to respectfully gather the wisdom of various world religions, moving from dialogue to designing and implementing the social, economic, and political public policy changes needed to save our world? For answers, let us look at a few dirty-hands ambiguities within some of the world's most beautiful religious value systems.

In Hinduism there are the *purusharthas*, or "values of life." One of these is *artha*, meaning "wealth," but this is not the capitalist individualized accumulation of wealth. Rather, *artha* is tied relationally to the ethical demands of *dharma* (duty). *Artha* is not to be pursued without the balancing ethical demand of *dharma*.[20]

The highest dharma virtue, *Paramo Dharma*, is best described as *ahimsa*, which literally means "no harm." The *a* signifies "not to be done," while *himsa* means "harm." *Ahimsa*, therefore, is a wonderfully short phrase that forms the central cosmological and moral mandate, so vast as to even "comprehend the whole created order."[21] The holy man Mohandas "Mahatma" Gandhi applied this ancient Hindu notion of *ahimsa* or "non-injury" to the concrete dirty-hands struggle of Indians for independence from British colonial expansion and control over the land of India. Gandhi developed a set of *ahimsa* practices that he called *satyagraha* (holding to the truth) as a nonviolence campaign to free all Indians (Hindu, Sikh, and Muslim) from the control of British colonialism. Now Hindus living in India (and its neighbors, Pakistan and Bangladesh) struggle to maintain the spirit of *satyagraha* as a self-governing people.

The practice of *ahimsa* is relevant to India's enormous population problem. Hindu doctrines and dictates are germane to preventing the environmental stresses caused by population exceedingly resources and opportunities. But *ahimsa* has even broader relevance in its potential for engendering a religious respect for the earth and its people and encouraging universal education, a factor directly related to all aspects of the population problem.[22]

Indians have also experienced the horrors of chemical spills. The infamous 1984 Union Carbide chemical spill in Bhopal killed and injured many people. The memories of this disaster remain fresh in the minds and hearts of Indians across the religious spectrum. A middle-way Journey ethic has the capacity to dialogue with Hindus on these issues respectfully, recognizing that we are all walking in solidarity toward less abusive environmental practices.

Islam has a strongly affirming view of the world. In Islam, the world is a place of innocence and good. Without evil in itself, the world has been made evil through the abuse of human beings.[23] The world is the theater for human service to Allah (God). According to Isma'il Al Faruqi, in Islam every act is capable of adding, however little, to the total value of the cosmos.[24] The earth, food, shelter, comfort, sex, reproduction, and all other "material things" are "to be enjoyed," but not to the point of abusing nature and Allah's creatures. The Koran commands, "Eat, drink, and enjoy yourselves, but do not abuse."[25] Thus, the ethics of Islam commands a persistent activism for the betterment of the world.[26] A Christian Journey ethics could learn much from such normative activism, joining ranks with Muslims in the reform of abusive environmental practices throughout the world. Christians can choose to be active in getting our hands dirty for the sake of cleansing a polluted world.

In autochthonous[27] or aboriginal religions—such as those of Native Americans, Australian Aborigines, and tribal peoples of Africa like the Akan of Ghana, West Africa—we find a deep reverence for and a sense of spiritual connection to the land, water, air, and creatures of the Earth. For many contemporary Westerners, it seems silly and superstitious to even speak about a profoundly mystical sense of connection to nature. For my particular construal of a Journey model of ethics, these religious systems offer modern Christianity a complex understanding of the nature of "natural communication," and they can teach us how to "communicate" with nature once again.

Before the Enlightenment's disenchantment of the world, even the most intelligent of Westerners believed in and practiced ways of living in which communing with nature, as something beyond the sum parts of its base resources, was commonplace. Now, after such practices have been debunked as "rubbish" for centuries, the West is going to have to relearn how to "feel," "hear," and "speak" to nature. The great mystics of Judaism, Islam, and Christianity seem to have never lost this mystical sense of communing with creation. Therefore, building on St. Francis's ability to name all things "brother" and "sister" and Thomas Merton's magnificent poetry communing with nature, the Journey model of ethics has great hope that the West can reconstruct a re-enchanted world of mystery and beauty in which to live, move, and have our being.

The basic teaching about our relationship to nature that the West has forgotten has to do with how much we human beings are a part of creation. Fundamentally, as the indigenous peoples of West Africa (Akan, Ewe, Fulani, Yoruba) would claim, human existence is "made possible through their [our] environment ." No well-adjusted individual can live "completely cut off from it [nature] . . . for such a person is sure to perish in the end."[28] What is at stake here? What is at stake is the realization that we can do more than merely "survive" ecocide; we can reconstrue a complicated, moral, intergenerational cosmology:

> [Survival] encompasses the world of ancestors and their relationships to nature; relationships which themselves provide the moral framework in terms of which members of the present generation define their own ways of dealing with each other and with nature.[29]

When we apply a profoundly relational view of the ties between past human ancestors, their cultural logics, and their capacity to affect our present cultural logics, nature becomes the necessary site of intergenerational ethical decision making. We are not concerned merely with what those who lived and died in the past practiced and believed, but we are also commended by our ancestors to remember the proper guidelines for choices every day. One frequently mentioned criterion in Native American religion urges that we act toward nature such that seven generations from now we shall still be remembered and honored for what we choose. This "seven generation ethical imperative" judges all ethical dilemmas, choices, and actions between humans and nature as regulated by a view toward the preservation of the Good, even seven generations later. Such a sanguine method of decision making has been shared by a huge variety of ethnicities, from the ancient Egyptians and Greeks to contemporary Native Americans and Australian Aboriginals.

What do we gain from returning to such an ancient ethical imperative of moral action? We gain a view of nature that guides our valuing of land, air, and water and that takes an incredibly conservative and long-range approach to using Gaia's resources. Further, it is ecumenical to the core, crossing the constricting boundaries of singularity such as "nationality" that have prevented human minds from conceiving of global solutions together. Our singular interest in a "religious" answer is pried open, forced to contemplate a multiplicity of ways that we can pragmatically (and paradigmatically) shift from conversations to public policy debates. We are called into the dirty realm of politics, working across our differences in order to communicate our beliefs in effective ways that have potential for being meaningful for an entire world.

One could go on naming the specific gifts and relevant contributions to be learned from Buddhism, Shinto, Confucianism, and many other magnificent expressions of human religiosity. The paradigm remains the same, a Journey model must move beyond the constrictions of a parochialized Christendom that judges all religious and ethical expressions other than its own to be inferior. On the Journey toward holiness those of us who call on Jesus as "Christ" are challenged to join in solidarity with all of God's creatures—no matter what religion, no matter what form of life (sentient and nonsentient, animals and plants, rocks and mountains, geysers and waterfalls). Our decisions must dance with the eagle and swim with the otter. They must be as quick as a cheetah and as protective of their young as the lioness. Such a view is deeply informed by the Eastern Orthodox, Ethiopian Coptic, and Roman Catholic traditions, not merely by one branch of Protestantism. All of these three Christian traditions hold to a highly *sacramental* view of life—that the Earth and all of her creatures are symbolic manifestations and incarnations of God's presence. A sacramental view of nature has traditionally been derided as mystical nonsense by most Enlightenment-informed, rationalized Protestants. This journey, however, calls us forward to a time when all of us will be challenged to learn some new skills, getting our hands dirty and deeming the Earth holy.

A FATHER'S LESSON. My father was a Jamaican immigrant, naturalized as an American citizen in the mid-1950s. He was the son of a plantation farmer, one of fifteen brothers and sisters. When he came to the United States of America, he learned how to be a factory machinist, but people of his "race" were not allowed to join the ranks of machinists at that time (even though he had very light-colored skin, and was even identified as "Jamaican White" on his visa). He became a factory line-worker, eventually operating the forklift that supplied the brake liner pads for one part of the line in a huge car assembly plant. Even with all of his acquaintance with the world of industry and the factory, he never lost his ability to "listen" to the Earth. He insisted that I learn how to do this, too, because it was a deep part of who he was. He taught me how to dig and plant, and together we planted well over a hundred blue spruce pines, Scotch pines, Japanese cherry trees, and various other plants, shrubs, and flowers on the two-acre plot of land that we called home. He would have me sit down on the rich black dirt of northern Ohio, and we would sink our fingers deep into the soil. We would quiet ourselves, and he would encourage me to "listen" with the palms of my hands and "feel the earth" with my fingertips. What was the soil "telling" us about this particular spot? Was it a good moist spot for planting a tree, or was it too soggy, or perhaps too dry? Was there water in the ground to feed the plant or tree after we had planted it? Perhaps most importantly, he taught me to recognize the Earth's attitude toward a plant. "Does the Earth want to support the life of this tree right here, or in another place?" Then he would say with deep reverence, "Feel the Earth," as we took our hands up off of the soil. "Rub it between your fingers. It is good."

All this might seem like hocus-pocus sentimentality, but for me there was a sacred quality about those times that I have never forgotten. Somehow my father seemed to "know" the Earth. He knew how to communicate with her. There was such a caressing quality to the way he touched the earth. He touched the dirt with the same gentle warmth with which he touched my mother's neck and kissed her on the cheek every night when he came home. So I connected dirt and soil with being feminine in some inarticulate symbolic space deeply tucked away in the back of my mind.

As my father caressed and "communicated" with the soil, so we must place our hands into the life-soil of our communities. What is the Earth under our feet and all around us challenging us to do? The entire community challenges us—whether it is cement-covered as a city street, grass-covered as a suburban expanse, tree-studded as a mountain range, or smog-infested as a Southern Californian valley. We are called to get dirty in order to become holy and to fulfill God's mission to the world through us. We do have the capacity to "communicate" with trees, rocks, mountains, water, and air; but we must be willing to unlearn the Lie of the Disenchanted Earth that the Enlightenment has postulated as truth. Some have worked so thoroughly at relearning this ancient form of "speech" that they speak of "experiencing warmth and love" while hugging a tree.[30] None of these kinds of nature-mystical experiences can become available to us until we have given up a mechanistic view of everything that is not human. Some may have read the Genesis 2 account of human "dominion" over nature as a call to detach ourselves from the Genesis 1 declaration that every aspect of nature and creation is "good," that the environment is a gift from God. In our time, in this particular historical moment of our great journey toward holiness known as following Jesus, our call to dominion is indeed a call for a more forward-looking stewardship of Earth's resources. In addition, we must reclaim the skill of listening unobtrusively in our communication with the Earth, even as we reach out to hear each other's human pleas for justice. Surely Gaia cries out for an end to the depletion of her ozone layer by our abuse of chlorofluorocarbons (CFCs), even if scientists cannot predict with absolute certainty whether or when global warming (or worse) might happen. But we have to listen to hear her.

If we have a seven generation ethical imperative, we followers of Christ cannot wait for scientific "certainty." We are summoned to find ways to change our heating and cooling technologies, to change our automobile habits, and to use them with the conviction of those called by God. With scientists fighting about the extent of damage that global warming will cause, most have settled into a consensus about global warming is an inevitable by-product of an industrialized, gasoline-driven world. Among the primary perpetrators of global warming are everyday automobile drivers, who produce the massive levels of CFCs, dioxins, lead, and other chemicals dumped into our air in the name of progress. That means that there is no escaping *our* responsibility for the death of the natural environment. So together, we must find ways to use fewer nonrenewable resources like gasoline, by traveling long distances less frequently, carpooling with neighbors, and the like. For some, this kind of commitment means total abstinence from cars, while for most, for whom the car has carefully modified their gasoline consumption.

Everybody has a role in reshaping agency, bringing forward a new definition of *dirtiness*. Dirty hands means that after our morning coffee, as we struggle to wear a cheerful "smile" on the way to the carpool, we recognize that the slight inconvenience of giving up our car to join a carpool is part of a large chorus of choices others are also making for cleaner air. As scientists work to counteract the possibly devastating rise in ocean sea levels, our dirty hands ethic urges us to fight for cleaner sources of energy for automobiles (ethanol, for example). Our hands will become dirty as we recalibrate our daily schedules so that we drive less and use less gasoline.

Every person has a part to play in creating a new contributive form of justice when it comes to cleaning up Gaia. Changing our national *habitus* of greed and individualism will not be easy. Such practices are deeply embedded in our cultures, whether we are black, brown, red, or white, poor or rich, homophobic or fully "affirming." Revaluing travel as something done in groups rather than in the privacy of an individual automobile may be the most difficult practice to change in the near future for most of us. For huge and wasteful multinational corporations, changing their *habitus* of greed will take much longer and will require greater perseverance and probably strong social and political intervention at some level. For example, the huge oil company Mobil has already found it very hard to "change over" from fossil fuels, so the emphasis in their television commercials from 1996 to1999 has been on creating "cleaner fuels," including the ethanol made by corn. Mobil may say that it wants cleaner gas, but its values and practices remain geared to the maximization of profits. With profits remaining the highest value, it will be interesting to see how alternative sources of energy compete with the traditional fuels. In the end, it may be that the amazing future will find Shell, Mobil, Exxon and the like becoming the new magnates of solar energy, ethanol, and wind power and the creators of more and more powerful batteries with quicker recharging times. These are resources that smaller companies are trying to develop now, but they have nothing like the resources of the oil "giants."

"DON'T WORRY, GET DIRTY!" I have rephrased the popular song "Don't Worry, Be Happy!" to suggest that contemporary holiness can be found in the simplest of places—a dirt pile, leaves, grass, and rocks. "Don't worry, get dirty!" invokes an earthy holiness that positively affirms our active integration of prayer with action. We pray for a cleaner environment, from South Los Angeles to South Boston, from San Diego to Miami. We pray for Arctic ice caps to stop melting and glaciers to stop disappearing. Yet since we already know that prayers cannot "work" unless we get our hands dirty, we choose to live out a holiness of listening, touching, and healing the Earth. Getting our physical hands dirty is holy. Further, it is the creation of a new spirituality that calls for peoples of all religions to put their hands and fingertips into the earth, and change her by working together with her and all of her creatures. Gaia is strong, but she needs our human solidarity to save her now. She requires the committed concrete actions of followers of Christ (and others) to engage in summoning back her full strength.

We find holiness in the actual feeling and touching of the Earth, feeling its language, and listening. There, under our feet, is an entire world of communication that we have only recognized by walking on Gaia's skin, cutting down her trees, and "developing" land that until now has been healthy because human touch has left it "undeveloped." There, in the silence of this moment, stop and listen. Do you hear the wind whispering? Are the waters dancing under your fingertips? Can you experience the warmth of a large rock placed in the midst of a carpet of plant vegetation? If we could only slow down and do these things for Gaia, how could we not also hear the cries of the poor, polluted, and toxically disenfranchised peoples living on Gaia? On our journey, the cries of Gaia and impoverished humanity are distinct, yet related to one larger reality.

NEW VALUES

Dirty Hands suggests several new ways of valuing the earth and our fellow human beings. Gifted enough to "hear" the Earth, we can certainly begin to express greater compassion for those whose communities are hemmed in by toxic waste processing plants. New values spring forth from this deeper connection to Gaia, others, and ultimately, ourselves. Key among these are the following:

- Treating each other as God's most precious gifts still remains singularly important to maintaining the fragility of Earth's natural processes.
- All creation is holy and valuable just as it is.
- All creatures of the Earth deserve a new home if displaced by human intervention. Such a home ought to be a setting that can sustain their lives just as they were before humans encroached on their territory. Many human creatures need to take much less space for our homes and to leave much more room for other creatures as part of the commonly shared space available for living.
- God calls followers of Jesus to be the teachers of "the Way," to communicate with created nature and with humanity about the sanctification of getting dirty and the blessing of acting with love and compassion.
- Jesus summons all of his followers to join hands, reach up, reach out, and then plunge our hands into the dirt of life, be it in a natural place, or in human relationships.
- Sanctification summons us into action, to lift our hands, reach them high, sweep them as low to the ground as possible, and then voice a blessing on the Earth and all of her creatures. Thus dirty hands are good hands, because dirt-is good.
- Abundant life is a gift of God for all persons, because all are created "in God's image."
- Planting, gardening, and cultivating soil is useful for us, because it reactivates our dulled appreciation for good dirt and for doing good for the Earth and for others.

Let us live into the dirtiness of real life, contemplating the gifts of holiness and the purity that is established in lives committed to acting as true followers of Jesus Christ.

FOR FURTHER REFLECTION

1. What rituals of reconnection with Gaia and each other would it be possible to create? Spend small-group study time on this task, and make

sure that you bring all the "supplies" you need to make a sensory-filled and interesting ritual!

2. How can we transform traditional Christian events (birth, baptism, marriage, etc.) into rituals of dirty hands healing?

3. What do you think about "communication," of any kind, with plants, rocks, trees, and water?

Notes

1. Professor Paris provided this description in a private conversation with me during my first attendance at an American Academy of Religion (AAR) Annual Meeting, in November 1991. He gently guided me through these approaches, speaking as a mentor would with a "greenhorn" in the field.

2. During a faculty presentation of a rough draft of this chapter my colleague Dan Rhoades made this claim. Davis Community Center, Claremont School of Theology, Claremont, Calif., September 20, 1996.

3. This approach might be called the "Harvard Divinity School" tradition, as it is shared by Preston Williams and his colleagues Ralph Potter and Arthur Dyck.

4. See Ralph Potter's *War and Moral Discourse* (Richmond: John Knox Press, 1973). Details of the Potter Box will be elaborated later.

5. I am particularly influenced here by Stanley Hauerwas's concern that holiness must be wedded to *truthful speech*. See his recent collection of essays, *Sanctify Them in the Truth: Holiness Exemplified* (Edinburgh: T & T Clark; Nashville, Tenn.: Abingdon Press, 1999).

6. I first encountered the term *diunital* in *Conjuring Culture* by Theophus Smith (Durham, NC: Duke University, 1994). My spouse, Karen, and I have also used the term to describe our theological and ethical methodology in *My Sister, My Brother: Womanist and Xodus God-Talk* (Maryknoll, N.Y.: Orbis, 1997).

7. For example, the "Jesus Project" of many noted New Testament scholars—including my colleagues Burton Mack, Gregory Riley, and Dennis R. MacDonald—aids and corrects assumptions about who Jesus really was.

8. This term is beautifully elaborated by Charles Kammer III in *Ethics and Liberation: An Introduction* (Maryknoll, N.Y.: Orbis, 1988) and by Daniel C. Maguire in various works, especially *The Moral Choice* (Garden City, N.Y.: Doubleday, 1978).

9. Alasdair MacIntyre, *After Virtue*, 2d ed. (South Bend, Ind.: University of Notre Dame Press, 1984).

10. Jeffrey Stout, *Ethics after Babel* (Boston: Beacon Press, 1988), p. 288.

11. Ibid., pp. 290–292.

12. Donald Bloesch, *Freedom for Obedience: Evangelical Ethics in Contemporary Times* (San Francisco: Harper & Row, 1987); Oliver O'Donovan, *Resurrection and Moral Order: An Outline for Evangelical Ethics* (Grand Rapids: Eerdmans, 1986); and Norman Geisler, *Christian Ethics* (Grand Rapids: Baker Book House, 1989).

13. "Strange as it may seem, [the] general conception of ethics coincides exactly with the conception of sin." Karl Barth, *Church Dogmatics*, II.2, trans. G. W. Bromiley, et al. (Edinburgh: T & T Clark, 1957), p. 518.

14. The psychological insights in this paragraph I owe to a colleague, Kathleen Greider. During faculty discussion of this chapter on September 20, 1996, at Claremont School of Theology, Greider informed me that according to object-relations theory (particularly the writings of Melanie Klein), the state of ambiguity is so discomforting to the psyche that one could conclude that living with ambiguity is an "acquired" state of "maturity." She further insisted that to ask persons to live on a perpetual "journey" is equally unhealthy, psychologically, because persons require both times of rest and times of movement.

15. Kammer, *Ethics and Liberation*, p. 8.

16. Such a characterization of deconstruction may be considered reductionist, but it is accurate from the perspective of a Christian love ethic. For a rich discussion of both the nihilist-relativist and the substantive aspects of Derrida and Emmanuel Levinas (as two representatives of deconstructive ethics), see Simon Critchley, *The Ethics of Deconstruction: Derrida and Levinas* (Oxford: Blackwell, 1992).

17. Michel Foucault's work on power as "power/knowledge" influences this aspect of my argument. For Foucault, power produces what becomes accepted as "truth," and this "power/knowledge" or "power/truth" has a ubiquitous capacity to embed itself pervasively in ordinary sociocultural and political relations. Michel Foucault, *Power/Knowledge: Selected Interviews and Other Writings, 1972–1977*, ed. Colin Gordon (New York: Pantheon, 1980).

18. Philosophical postmodernist theologian David R. Griffin has often voiced this criticism to me in conversations throughout 1997 and 1998.

19. This last idea arose in response to a faculty discussion by Lori Anne Ferrell, who suggested that perhaps I ought not call the Journey love ethic *deconstructive*, or that I should find a way to incorporate deconstructive suspicion into a new kind of postmodernism. I opted to do the latter.

CHAPTER 2

1. Paul Ramsey, *Basic Christian Ethics* (Chicago: University of Chicago Press, 1950), p. xi.

2. Ibid., p. xii.

3. One might think that this is merely an extreme example of Christian ethics, practiced most strongly in conservative Christian churches, but I take it to be an essential aspect of the mainstream, too.

4. All quotes from the previous two paragraphs taken from David Clark and Robert Rakestraw, *Readings in Christian Ethics*, vol. 1, *Theory and Method* (Grand Rapids: Baker House, 1994), p. 64.

5. Definitions in this paragraph are built on those provided in Charles Kammer III, *Ethics and Liberation: An Introduction* (Maryknoll, N.Y.: Orbis, 1988), pp.26–28.

6. Bruce C. Birch and Larry Rasmussen, *Bible and Ethics in the Christian Life* (Minneapolis: Augsburg, 1989), pp. 66–67.

7. Ibid., p. 74.

8. Ibid., p. 75.

9. This internalization of selected aspects of our communal moral legacy is what makes it possible for us to celebrate the actions of a few committed white Americans in participating in the Underground Railroad that freed slaves even though the United States legally sanctioned slavery at the time (the nineteenth century). It is also what makes it possible for us to celebrate various Catholic and Protestant Europeans of deep moral conviction who hid Jews during the Nazi genocide of European Jewry during World War II.

10. Ibid., p. 81.

11. For more detailed information about Augustine and Luther, see Robin Gill, *A Textbook of Christian Ethics* (Edinburgh: T & T Clark, 1985), pp. 1983–2223, 330–343; see also Timothy F. Lull, *Martin Luther's Basic Theological Writings* (Minneapolis: Fortress, 1989), pp. 218–220, 655–703.

12. Clark and Rakestraw, *Theory and Method*, p. 139.

13. This example of courage is found in Aristotle's *Nichomachaean Ethics*.

14. I use the term *race* out of social concession, recognizing that the rhetoric of race is a peculiarly destructive social practice that negates the concrete biogenetic fact that there is only *one* race—the human race.

15. Clark and Rakestraw, *Theory and Method*, p. 18.

16. Ibid.

17. Ibid.

18. For further information, see Karl Barth, *Church Dogmatics*, II.1, *Epistle to the Romans*, trans. by Edwin Hoskyns, 6th ed. (London: Oxford University Press, 1968), and *Church Dogmatics*, III.4.

19. Stanley Hauerwas admits his strong Barthian influence and informs my thinking here on Barth's critics. "Barth provides extensive discussions of such matters as suicide, euthanasia, marriage and singleness, the ethics of war, the Christian calling to serve the neighbor, but denies that casuistry can ever predetermine 'God's concrete and specific command here and now in this particular way, of making a corresponding decision.' Accordingly Barth's ethics is often criticized for being too 'occasionalistic,' since he denies that we can ever predetermine what we should do prior to God's command." Stanley Hauerwas, *Sanctify Them in the Truth: Holiness Exemplified* (Edinburgh: T & T Clark, 1998), p. 34.

20. Reinhold Niebuhr, *Moral Man and Immoral Society* (New York: Macmillan, 1932); *The Nature and Destiny of Man*, 2 vols. (Louisville, Ky.: Westminster John Knox Press, 1996).

21. H. Richard Niebuhr, *The Responsible Self: An Essay in Christian Moral Philosophy* (New York: Harper & Row, 1963).

22. See John B. Cobb Jr., *Sustainability* (Maryknoll, N.Y.: Orbis, 1994); and *Sustaining the Common Good* (Cleveland: Pilgrim, 1994); David Ray Griffin's SUNY series—*God and Religion in the Postmodern World: Essays in Postmodern Theology* (Albany: SUNY Press, 1989), *The Reenchantment of Science: Postmodern Proposals* (Albany: SUNY Press, 1988), *Spirituality and Society: Postmodern Visions* (Albany: SUNY Press, 1988), and *Sacred Interconnections: Postmodern Spirituality, Political Economy, and Art* (Albany: SUNY Press, 1990).

23. Cited in Louis P. Pojman, *Ethical Theory: Classical and Contemporary Readings* (Belmont, Calif.: Wadsworth Publishing Co., 1995), p. 726.

24. Thomas Aquinas, *Summa Theologiae*, II, Q. 7, art. 1, as quoted in Gill, *Textbook of Christian Ethics*, p. 78.

25. S. Cromwell Crawford, *Global Religions and Global Ethics* (New York: Paragon, 1989), p. 5.

26. Ibid., p. 226.

27. Zygmunt Bauman, *Postmodern Ethics* (Oxford: Blackwell, 1993), pp. 10–11.

28. Ibid., p. 11.

29. Ibid., p. 12.

30. Ibid., p. 13.

31. Ibid., pp. 13–14.

32. Ibid., pp. 14–15.

33. Dietrich Bonhoeffer, *A Testament of Freedom: The Essential Writings of Dietrich Bonhoeffer*, ed. Geffrey Kelly and Burton Nelson (San Francisco: HarperSanFrancisco, 1990), p. 368.

34. Ibid., p. 363.

35. Ibid., p. 367.

36. Ibid.

37. Ibid., p. 324.

38. Ibid., p. 325.

39. Ibid., p. 32.

CHAPTER 3

1. Ralph Potter, *War and Moral Discourse* (Richmond, Va.: John Knox Press, 1973).

2. Ibid., pp. 23–24, as quoted in Charles Kammer III, *Ethics and Liberation: An Introduction* (Maryknoll, N.Y.: Orbis, 1988), pp. 17–18.

3. Kammer, *Ethics and Liberation*, pp. 19–20.

4. Ibid., p. 20.

5. Ibid., pp. 23–26.

6. Ibid., p. 28.

7. Ibid., p. 31.

8. Ibid., pp. 33–34.

9. My articulation of these two questions is based on Geisler's two "distinguishing characteristics of Christian ethics." *Christian Ethics: Options and Issues* (Grand Rapids: Baker Book House, 1989), pp. 22–23.

10. This insight can be gained from a close reading of Oliver O'Donovan's underlying doctrine of God in *Resurrection and Moral Order: An Outline for Evangelical Ethics* (Grand Rapids: Eerdmans, 1986). Such a claim, of course, is unashamedly Christian.

11. Bruce Birch and Larry Rasmussen, *Bible and Ethics in the Christian Life*, revised and expanded edition (Minneapolis: Augsburg, 1989), p. 40. The inspiration for the section I call "moral metaphysics" comes from this book, as does the definition of "moral agency." See pp. 39–40.

12. Ibid., p. 40.

13. David Couzens Hoy and Thomas McCarthy, *Critical Theory* (Oxford: Blackwell, 1994), pp. 16, 19.

14. Craig Calhoun, *Critical Social Theory* (Oxford: Blackwell, 1995), p. 35.

15. Ibid., p. 51.

16. Pierre Bourdieu, *Outline of a Theory of Practice*, trans. Richard Nice (Cambridge: Cambridge University Press, 1977), p. 72.

17. Ibid., p. 78.

18. Pierre Bourdieu, *The Field of Cultural Production: Essays on Art and Literature*, ed. and introduced by Randal Johnson (Oxford: Colombia Press, 1993), p. 4.

19. Ibid., p. 6.

20. All quotes in this paragraph, ibid., pp. 6–7.

21. Ibid., p. 7.

22 Arthur Dyck, *Rethinking Rights and Responsibilities: The Moral Bonds of Community* (Cleveland: Pilgrim Press, 1994), pp. 14–15.

23. Ibid., pp. 331–332.

24. Ibid., pp. 331–32.

25. Kammer, *Ethics and Liberation*, pp. 35–52.

26. Ibid., pp. 54 ff.

27. Daniel Day Williams, "God and Man," in *Process Theology*, ed. Ewert H. Cousins (New York: Newman Press, 1971), p. 182.

28. John B. Cobb Jr., "The World and Man," in Cousins, *Process Theology*, pp. 166–128.

29. Marjorie Suchocki provides an excellent example of this extension of Walter Rauschenbusch's argument in *The Fall to Violence* (New York: Continuum, 1994).

30. See Rabbi Joseph Telushkin, *Jewish Literacy: The Most Important Things to Know about the Jewish Religion, Its People, and Its History* (New York: William Morrow & Company, 1991), pp. 154–155.

CHAPTER 4

1. Thomas Aquinas, *Summa of the Summa: The Essential Philosophical Passages of St. Thomas Aquinas' Summa Theologica Edited and Explained for Beginners*, ed. Peter Kreeft (San Francisco: Ignatius Press, 1990), pp. 465-466.

2. Thomas Aquinas, *Summa*, II–II, q. 25, art. iv, as quoted in H. Richard Niebuhr and Waldo Beach, *Christian Ethics*, 2nd ed. (New York: John Wiley & Sons, 1973), pp. 222–223.

3. Niebuhr and Beach, *Christian Ethics*, p. 222.

4. Paul Tillich, *Love, Power, and Justice* (New York: Oxford University Press, 1954), p. 33.

5. Ibid., p. 27.

6. The popular musician "Formerly Known as 'Prince'" used to chant this over and over again in his early music in the 1980s.

7. For all references in this paragraph, see Anders Nygren, *Agape and Eros*, trans. Philip S. Watson (Chicago: University of Chicago Press, 1953).

8. Cited in Ibid., pp. 606–607.

9. Ibid., p. 617.

10. Ibid., p. 619.

11. Ibid., p. 621.

12. Ibid., p. 662, citing Luther, "Temporal Authority."

13. Ibid., p. 663.

14. Ibid., p. 664.

15. Ibid., p. 668.

16. Ibid., p. 668.

17. Ibid., p. 670.

18. Ibid., pp. 699–700.

19. Martin Luther, *Whether Soldiers, Too, Can Be Saved*, in Robin Gill, *A Textbook of Christian Ethics* (Edinburgh, Scotland: T & T Clark, 1985), p. 334.

20. Ibid., p. 335.

21. Ibid.

22. Ibid., pp. 338–339.

23. Karen Lebacqz, *Six Theories of Justice* (Minneapolis: Augsburg, 1986), p. 21.

24. Ibid., p. 40.

25. Ibid., p. 56.

26. Ibid., pp. 70–75.

27. Ibid., pp. 91–96

28. Ibid., pp. 108–109.

29. Starhawk, *Truth or Dare: Encounters with Power, Authority, and Mystery* (New York: Harper & Row, 1987).

30. Walter Rauschenbusch, *Christianity and the Social Crisis* (Louisville, Ky.: Westminster John Knox Press, 1991), pp. 42, 67.

31. Walter Rauschenbusch, *A Theology for the Social Gospel*, p. 68.

32. Nygren, *Agape and Eros*, pp.75–81.

33. Martin Luther King Jr., *Stride toward Freedom* (New York: Harper & Row, 1957), p. 19; and *A Testament of Hope: The Essential Writings and Speeches of Martin Luther King, Jr.*, ed. James Melvin Washington (San Francisco), pp. 19–20.

34. Martin Luther King Jr., "Letter from Birmingham Jail," in *A Testament of Hope*, p. 293.

35. Martin Luther King Jr., *Where Do We Go from Here?* in *A Testament of Hope*, p. 577.

36. Ibid., p. 578.

37. Ibid.

38. For Rauschenbusch, see nn. 30, 31 above; for Reinhold Niebuhr, see esp. *The Nature and Destiny of Man*, 2 vols. (N.Y.: Charles Scribner's Sons, 1941, 1943); for Martin Luther King Jr., see above, n. 33; for Beverly W. Harrison, see *Making the Connections: Essays in Feminist Social Ethics*, ed. Carol S. Robb (Boston: Beacon, 1985); for Emilie M. Townes, *In a Blaze of Glory: Womanist Spirituality as Social Witness* (Nashville: Abingdon, 1995).

CHAPTER 5

1. Emilie Townes, *In a Blaze of Glory* (Nashville: Abingdon Press, 1995) pp. 80–84; and in the Martin Luther King Jr. Lecture, Claremont School of Theology, February 1995.

2. See Marie Fortune, *Love Does No Harm: Sexual Ethics for the Rest of Us* (New York: Continuum, 1995).

CHAPTER 6

1. The modern West struggles with the Greco-Roman philosophical and symbolic legacy that has associated *light* with *good, right, clean* and *dark* with *evil, wrong, dirty.*

2. All of the above quotations come from John Wesley's *A Plain Account of Christian Perfection*, excerpted in J. Philip Wogaman and Douglas M. Strong, eds., *Readings in Christian Ethics: A Historical Sourcebook* (Louisville, Ky.: Westminster John Knox Press, 1996), pp. 175–176.

3. Ibid., p. 177. After long years of observing the variety of human capacities for growing in holiness, Wesley noted that this was generally a "gradual work" that both preceded and followed instantaneous justification (being made right before God in conversion). Yet he contradicted himself in the following paragraph by insisting that the very "instant" of perfection was "the instant of death, the moment before the soul leaves the body."

4. The idea of God calling us into an "adventure" originates with Alfred North Whitehead, especially in his *Adventures in Ideas.* John Cobb Jr.'s taped address to his colleagues at Claremont School of Theology on May 13, 1994, ended with this challenge: "Adventure forth in God!"

5. Levinas's enigmatic and prophetic call for "responsibility" that is rooted in actual face-to-face encounters with others is one of his fundamental moral philosophical themes. See *Of God Who Comes to Mind*, trans. Bettina Bergo (Stanford, Calif.: Stanford University Press, 1998), pp. 8–14, 111–121. See also Emmanuel Levinas, "Ethics as First Philosophy," in *The Levinas Reader*, ed. Sean Hand (Oxford: Blackwell, 1998 reprint), pp. 75–87.

7. This joining together of what Reinhold Niebuhr called "nature and history" with the "transcendent ideal" of God's love is a theme he first mentioned in "The Relevance of an Impossible Ethical Ideal," in *An Interpretation of Christian Ethics* (New York: Harper & Row, 1935), p. 245. In *From Christ to the World,* he elaborates the same ideals much more cogently (although he never again examines the notion of God's love as a necessary yet "impossible" ethical *telos*).

8. Recent works such as McFague's *Super, Natural Christians* (Minneapolis: Fortress Press, 1997) articulate an elaborate "theology of nature" that is much more expansive than that found in the earlier writings of Rosemary Radford Ruether. Ruether's continuing growth in this area has pushed her to listen and include various women's voices on ecological healing from the First and Third Worlds. See, for example, *Women Healing Earth* (Maryknoll, N.Y.: Orbis, 1997).

9. An interesting and thought provoking movie titled *GATTACA* imagines a society that completely controls its genetic development. This society eventually becomes a scientifically based form of discrimination between those who "belong" and those who do not.

10. Cynthia Hamilton, "Women, Home and Community: The Community in an Urban Environment," in *Re-Weaving the World: The Emergence of Ecofeminism,* ed. Irene Diamond and Gloria Felman Orenstein (San Francisco: Sierra Club Books, 1990), p. 216.

11. Charles Lee, "Beyond Toxic Wastes and Race," in *Confronting Environmental Racism: Voices from the Grassroots,* ed. Robert D. Bullard (Boston: South End Press, 1993), p. 50.

12. Ibid., p. 50.

13. Hamilton, "Women, Home and Community," p. 216.

14. Dioxin and mercury are two of the most dangerous chemical pollutants found by waste sites.

15. Hamilton, "Women, Home and Community," p. 216. This comment was made by Charlotte Bullock, who noted that "common sense" was sufficient; she did not need to be a "rocket scientist" to be suspicious.

16. Ibid., p. 220.

17. Robert Bullard, "Anatomy of Environmental Racism and the Environmental Justice Movement," in *Confronting Environmental Racism,* p. 21.

18. *Race* is a modern Western misnomer for *ethnicity* and is used quite effectively in isolating darker skinned peoples to an inferior, second-class citizenship within the very heart of egalitarian "modern" Enlightened ideals.

19. Pollution travels with us even as we try to escape it. The television news program *20/20* (August 13, 1999) reported shocking statistics about how toxic and unhealthy our national forests and parks are.

20. S. Cromwell Crawford, "Hindu Ethics for Modern Life," in *World Religions and Global Ethics* (New York: Paragon House, 1989), p. 31.

21. Ibid., p. 14. Such a comprehensive application of the term reminds one of the Hebraic Torah, or God's Law, and the tripartite definition of "law" (eternal, natural, and human) developed by Thomas Aquinas.

22. Ibid., p.26.

23. Isma'il R. Al Faruqi, "Islamic Ethics," in Crawford, *World Religions and Global Ethics*, p. 227.

24. Ibid., p. 228.

25. Ibid. Al Faruqi lists *surahs* from the Koran in his accompanying footnote 37, p. 237, "Qur'an 7:18; 2:57, 60, 168, 172; 7:159; 20:81; 6:142; 16:114; 5:91; 23L52; 34:15; 52:19; 69:24; 77:43; and 4:3."

26. Ibid., p. 229.

27. *Autochthonous* refers to the original peoples who traditionally inhabited and arose from a particular land.

28. John K. Ansah, "The Ethics of African Religious Traditions," in Crawford, *World Religions and Global Ethics*, p. 261.

29. Edward P. Antonio, "Letting People Decide: Towards an Ethics of Ecological Survival in Africa," in *Ecotheology: Voices from South and North*, ed. David G. Halliman (Maryknoll, N.Y.: Orbis, 1994), p. 231.

30. This is one of Professor Howard Clinebell's extraordinary claims in *Ecotherapy: Healing Ourselves, Healing the Earth* (Minneapolis: Fortress Press, 1996).

Index